Argentina under the Kirchners

Praise for the book

'This important book presents a highly readable, timely and definitive analysis of twelve years of Kirchnerism. It is essential reading for those who want to understand the dynamics behind how popular and successful left-wing governments are defeated and conservative administrations elected to replace them in Argentina and potentially other parts of Latin America.'

Daniel Ozarow, Senior Lecturer at Middlesex University and Co-Chair of the Argentina Research Network

'This is a lucid and effective analysis of the Kirchner regimes in Argentina. Covering a remarkable range but always in clear and elegant prose, this achieves the significant feat of a balanced evaluation of a period that became so contentious and polarized. We come to understand better the politics, economics and political culture of the Kirchner period, and the reasons both for its end and for many of its successes. An impressive achievement.'

Sian Lazar, Department of Archaeology and Anthropology, University of Cambridge

Argentina under the Kirchners
The legacy of left populism

Marcela López Levy

LAB
LATIN AMERICA BUREAU

PRACTICAL ACTION
Publishing

Published by Practical Action Publishing Ltd in association with Latin America Bureau
The Schumacher Centre,
Bourton on Dunsmore,
Rugby, Warwickshire,
CV23 9QZ, UK
www.practicalactionpublishing.org

Latin America Bureau,
Enfield House, Castle Street,
Clun, Shropshire,
SY7 8JU, UK
www.lab.org.uk
© Marcela López Levy, 2017

A catalogue record for this book is available from the British Library.
A catalogue record for this book has been requested from the Library of Congress.
ISBN 9781909014053 Paperback
ISBN 9781909014084 Library Ebook
ISBN 9781909014060 Ebook

Citation: López Levy, Marcela., (2017) *Argentina under the Kirchners: The legacy of left populism*, Rugby, UK: Practical Action Publishing, <http://dx.doi.org/10.3362/9781909014084>

Since 1974, Practical Action Publishing has published and disseminated books and information in support of international development work throughout the world. Practical Action Publishing is a trading name of Practical Action Publishing Ltd (Company Reg. No. 1159018), the wholly owned publishing company of Practical Action. Practical Action Publishing trades only in support of its parent charity objectives and any profits are covenanted back to Practical Action (Charity Reg. No. 247257, Group VAT Registration No. 880 9924 76).

Latin America Bureau (Research and Action) Limited is a UK registered charity (No.1113039). Since 1977 LAB has been publishing books, news, analysis and information about Latin America, reporting consistently from the perspective of the region's poor, oppressed or marginalized communities and social movements. In 2015 LAB entered into a publishing partnership with Practical Action Publishing.

Cover design by Andrew Corbett
Typeset by Allzone Digital Services Ltd.
Printed in the United Kingdom

Contents

http://dx.doi.org/10.3362/9781909014084.000

Contents

CHAPTER ONE
Introduction: populism, Peronism and the rift

Remember when politics was about the economy, and if you didn't agree you were stupid? Argentina in the period 2003 to 2015 proves that there's more to it than that. The country had a booming economy until 2008, and more modest expansion thereafter, but nothing like the austerity and recession seen in richer countries. And yet the 2015 elections were won on the promise of 'Change' ('Cambiemos'– the slogan of the winning coalition). What changes were people clamouring for?

In 2013 President Cristina Fernández de Kirchner (CFK) made a speech about what had been achieved under her rule, and that of her husband Néstor before her. She called it the 'decade gained', in contrast to what had been lost to neoliberalism in the 1990s, and the 'lost decade' of crippling debt of the 1980s. Howls of media derision met her claim of a decade won, and it was clear that a large sector of the population was not happy with the advances made. How to explain the discontent?

'Who gained what?' is perhaps the central political question anywhere, and in Argentina the answers are surprising. Between the years of 2003 and 2015 the poor gained work, social protection, consumer credit; the middle class gained reinforced labour rights, wage rises above inflation, cheap consumer credit and subsidised travel[1]; exporters were able to exploit the favourable international conditions and make use of state-funded infrastructure; multinationals were able to make profits

http://dx.doi.org/10.3362/9781909014084.001

in key sectors (mining, energy, car production); the press was free to publish what it saw fit; the state gained employees and doubled the tax base; inequality fell for the first time in 20 years, contrary to trends elsewhere in the world; the number of new cars soared, motorway mileage tripled and housing was built and renovated at a tremendous pace. Schools were constructed and spending in education reached 6 per cent of GDP, with much of it going to teachers and training.

So who were the losers? Why the derision when CFK took credit for the gains of the decade? In economic terms, the pace of inflation, between 20 and 30 per cent from 2009 onwards hurt the poor most. But they were not the ones protesting loudly against the government. It was the rich with access to dollars (who benefited from inflation, which made things cheaper for them in pesos) who were most vocal in their discontent. The 'losers' did not lose economic power. But they did lose control over the political process and feared that the economic gains of the poor and working people would make it impossible to regain power. The actions of the wealthiest were restricted in some areas: importers needed licenses; currency controls made it harder to take dollars out of the country; restricted imports meant less choice in consumer goods. Yet this doesn't seem enough to explain the visceral dislike CFK aroused.

A growing number of people felt that important, if intangible, things were lost during the rule of the Kirchners: the ability to voice dissent while remaining broadly in agreement with the aims of the government; the chance to debate and have reliable and constructive arguments around major policy decisions; the possibility of having a plurality of opinion. Even though the nation, and the national interest, were themes repeated throughout the 12 years they governed, there was little sense of national unity, of everyone 'being in it together'. Even though the majority benefited from government actions, the Kirchner project was voted out of office by half of the population. The vote against CFK's chosen successor had more to do with weariness and alarm at the levels of antagonism in society than with unhappiness with the concrete results of the Kirchners' 12 years in government.

The Kirchners saw the state as an engine of economic growth, allocating capital and work to developmental and strategic aims, but the way resources were distributed was politically-driven and increasingly benefited a small number of loyal businesses via trusted officials. The issue of corruption became a key weapon for the opposition, although unfortunately there is no prospect of a truly independent judiciary to tackle the endemic culture of impunity that permeates public life in Argentina. What *The Economist* calls 'crony capitalism' was not created by the governments of Kirchner and CFK – it is a central mechanism in how the private sector interacts with the state across the ideological spectrum. President Macri's family fortune grew from state contracts.[2] And in the same way that transparency and institution building were not priorities in the political arena, neither were they in the economic realm. Economic decisions involving the government were made in unaccountable ways that made misappropriation possible.

Three approaches

But how to understand what went on in Argentina under the Kirchners and what has happened since? Clearly this short account of what took place during the governments of Néstor Kirchner (2003-2007) and

Cristina Fernández de Kirchner (2007-2015) cannot do justice to all the events of the period. I am proposing three ways in to making sense of the period, three ways of looking at a turbulent time. The three themes outlined below are: populism, 1970s Peronism, and the 'rift' (*la grieta*³), the split in society that polarises public discourse. These are all complex issues in their own right, so clarifying what I mean by them will, I hope, help to make anything else you read on Argentina more intelligible.

1. Left populism

Although the word populism means 'of the people', it is a style of politics with a bad reputation. It tends to be used to disparage politics per se and to describe politicians who pander to prejudice. But populism is also the politics that appeals to people's lived experience, and recognises that many votes are not cast for rational reasons, but in response to a mix of identification and aspiration. In Europe we are familiar with right-wing populism, the narratives that blame the most vulnerable, often with racist arguments, for economic and political problems. The populism of the Kirchners was left-wing because its rhetoric took aim at the wealthiest – in their political pitch it was the rich who betrayed the national interest of workers and pensioners. The appeal of left-wing populism for progressive politics is that it focuses on the welfare of ordinary working people. Ernesto Laclau, a political theorist who became a favoured thinker for Kirchnerist politics, argued that populism is a way of doing politics (not an ideology) that includes more people in the political process, extending democracy. Laclau also argued that for populism to be successful it needs to build its strength by mobilising people to stand against vested interests.

This confrontational aspect of the left-wing populist approach to politics, of making the rich and powerful the enemy of the people, brought divisions to the fore in unintended ways.

The progressive project of expanding democracy under left-populism was limited by the selective support for some rights over others. Social and economic rights were prioritised, and social and economic gains did occur: Kirchner and CFK's governments promoted an array of policies to provide economic inclusion – for the unemployed, the informally employed and pensioners – that is, for the greater portion of citizens who had seen their income decline under neoliberalism in the 1990s. They also supported greater legal rights for women workers, for homosexual couples who wanted to marry, and for transgender people who wanted their chosen identity to be recognized. Less tangibly than through laws and pensions, the climate of openness to social organizing and demands, and the re-cycling of the Peronist idea of 'dignity', worked to enable the expansion of tolerance. The evidence for that sense of possibility was provided by the people who spontaneously turned up at Plaza de Mayo to say goodbye to CFK on her last day in power in 2015. They wanted to thank her for the possibility of being more themselves, of being less afraid to demand respect.

However, in situations where social rights clashed with economic interests, ordinary people often lost out. Many indigenous communities suffered violence when they tried to resist land grabs, and entire villages were attacked when they protested against mining projects.[4] Ongoing environmental problems that affected communities were not tackled when they meant challenging profitable enterprises such as soya growing or petrochemicals.[5] Anthropologist Javier Auyero has traced the lives of those affected by chemical pollution in shantytowns near Buenos Aires. His recent work, *Patients of the State*,[6] showed that even if there were improvements to the lives of the poorest, these were too little, and sometimes too late. In what he calls 'the politics of waiting', he shows how people's struggle to improve their lives is fuelled by a tenacious determination that state institutions mostly try to thwart.

But even where economic and social inclusion succeeded, it was by means of discretionary measures. There was no consistent programme to make institutions more responsive and protest remained the main route to political involvement. Elections were fair and clean (voting is compulsory). But the way political decisions were taken was mainly by a small group of loyal aides and ministers, supporting highly executive decisions taken by the President. Political initiatives were put to Congress, but its role as a counter balance was limited, by the long-standing habit of presidential recourse to executive powers, by the inability of the opposition to unite during the best part of the period 2003-2015, and by the working majorities the government enjoyed in both houses of Congress from 2005 to 2015. The other source of countervailing power, the judiciary, has historically lacked the independence needed to be a true check on the executive.

What does all this have to do with populism? It has to do with the idea that those elected connect with the electorate and become active defenders of a vision that needs no further consultation. At best, populism has the potential for including those least able economically to make their political voice heard on the national stage. At worst, it takes it upon itself to voice the will of all the people. This worked for Néstor Kirchner when people wanted the reassurance of a clear path ahead after the chaos of financial meltdown in 2001; but by the time CFK came to power in 2007, her assumption that her actions were in everyone's best interests began to grate with many.

Speaking for others is a model of leadership that has served politics well in representative democracies. Perón himself and his wife Evita, set a high bar for creating political personas with whom the majority could identify. But it also alienates those who want a voice, who want transparency and a system of decision-making that is accountable. Many people felt silenced and sidelined in the political process created by the Kirchners. For those with different political ideas, or who did not agree with how these were put into practice, being 'spoken for' became a frustration and sometimes led to anger, an anger that first erupted in the protests against the government in 2008. Increasing taxes for agribusiness should have been a popular measure – and yet thousands mobilized in support of wealthy exporters? The 'shock and awe' approach to policy change used by Kirchner and then CFK alienated many and led to popular sympathy with some of the most powerful landowners in the country.

Yet the Kirchners were caught in a political paradox not of their making. The Argentinian electorate demands strong leadership and is scathing of weakness and ineffectiveness – a double fault laid at the door of President Fernando de la Rua (1999-2001). The imperative to be a strong leader is a long-standing feature of political life and leaders are damned if they do and damned if they don't. To put the contradictory demands of the electorate into historical perspective, in the recent commemorations of the coup against one of the few democratic presidents of the 1960s, Arturo Illia (1963-1966), the writer Marcos Aguinis[7] recalls: 'the successes of his austere and dynamic administration were sabotaged with a hostility that now seems incredible, absurd. There was a delirious intention to get him out of power at any price, who knows why. The

thinking media did not value the extent of his patrio-
tism or his lucid statesmanship. Ramiro de Casasbellas,
a journalist of *Primera Plana* who ceaselessly defamed
him, acknowledged later that 'the government of
Arturo Illia did not abuse power an inch; the reserve
of his mandate we called "power vacuum"; the observance of the law "democratic formality"; his modera-
tion "slowness"; his silent and correct work, with no
showy self-promotion, "inefficiency"; the repudiation
of demagoguery, "sectarianism"; his spirit of consensus "lack of authority"; and the severe defence of
national, popular and Christian doctrine "rule by committee". We were the sectarian ones, the ones without
authority.'

Some might balk at portraying the Kirchners in the
saintly light that Illia's three years in power now attracts,
but his experience is illuminating: the imperative to be
seen to be effective while the behaviour of the media
and the failings of individuals undermine polices, is the
impossible task facing presidents. Neither is conducive
to a critical and sober evaluation of government. The
Kirchners were in power much longer than Illia and
undoubtedly were far more powerful. Yet the reaction-
ary opinions in the media and among the middle-class
that undermined Illia went unchallenged then, and
remain a destructive force in politics to this day.

The Kirchners were as aware as anyone that politics is
an unforgiving business and concentrated on accumu-
lating power and resources to see their political project
through. Getting things done, being effective, is one of
the traits associated with Peronist leadership, and the
Kirchners played up to it, ensuring things were done, or
claiming they were. Many were put off by *how* they got
them done, but the critics often confused means and
ends. For the Kirchners, the ends justified the means.

Yet those who disagreed with them contributed to polarized arguments by opposing their objectives, not just the way they pursued them. All nuance was lost. The element of surprise favoured by Néstor Kirchner and then CFK for presenting policies became akin to landing the first punch.

This brings us to the economics of the left-populism espoused by the Kirchners. In line with their pragmatism, in order to get things done, to have people follow them and obey them, they needed money: money for the state to invest and distribute, and money of their own to campaign with. In Argentina there is no control over campaign spending, nor over government spending on advertising. One key source of money came from what Neal Richardson has called 'export-oriented populism'[8] – both Kirchners allowed large exporting interests to thrive in order to increase government revenue for infrastructure and social spending. Yet the support for large economic interests could not be made transparent, when Peronist rhetoric was blaming these same interests for acting against the nation and the people.

Some clues as to what they really meant can be found in the assessment made by the President of the Chamber of Imports, Diego Pérez Santisteban. When he was asked to describe the Kirchner era in keywords: he said, 'model, administered commerce, unpredictability and lack of written rules'.[9] The 'model' was the term used by Néstor Kirchner to describe his economic policy of state-led development with a strong export sector. The model was one where the government placed itself as a force to be reckoned with in the economy, using its power to direct investment and bully companies whose business reduced the balance of trade. But the crucial aspect of the model was the 'unwritten rules', the changeable and discretionary political favour, where relationships were paramount.

The wider economic picture, of a reaction against neo-liberalism, a return to economic sovereignty and state-led development was significant in the questions raised: is the economy about finance or production? How much sovereignty can countries negotiate with international finance? These are important questions for all countries, and especially for developing nations. The Kirchners did not have all the answers, but a critical approach to the power of finance versus the power of national governments is a debate ignored in other countries at the peril of democracy. In the IMF report *'Neoliberalism: Oversold?'*[10] researchers wonder if the economic measures it espoused had not caused more harm than good. It is not yet common sense to reject crippling debt and market solutions for social problems, but Argentina was the first G20 country to challenge the consensus. While the developed

Cristina & Nestor Kirchner embrace before the crowd in the Plaza de Mayo, June 2008
Presidencia de la Nación Argentina. Creative Commons Attribution 2.0 Generic

economies headed for the crash of 2008 and have failed to recover their dynamism afterwards, during the same time Argentina's economy was growing and redistributing wealth. There were many flaws in how this was done, and the shortcomings created inflation and instability. But the aim of redistributing wealth to the poor, to the workers, to the old and the young, was real and concrete steps were taken in that direction. The market ideology of neoliberalism, of winner takes all, was contested by the Kirchners – only partially, but enough to show that neoliberalism is a policy choice, and that other choices are possible. In a hostile international environment, the open pursuit of such policies was attacked from many sides.

The Kirchners practised a left-populism that made the poor, the unemployed, the old and the young, into the national identity, into 'us', and the traditional ruling class of landowners, transnational companies and the media into 'them'. At least rhetorically. In practice, landowners made record profits, the bulk of transnational companies prospered (only the exceptions made the news), the media was free, and free to be extremely critical of the government, while the middle class enjoyed rising salaries, subsidized services and holidays.

2. Peronism once again

So how did populism and Peronism intersect? Both Néstor Kirchner and Cristina Fernández de Kirchner were long-standing members of the Justicialist Party (PJ) founded by Juan Domingo Perón in the 1940s. They became Peronists as students during the 1970s, when the Peronist movement was deeply divided between a right-wing led by Perón himself (who died in 1975) and a left-wing that contained social organizations and an armed insurgency, the Montoneros.

The first period of Peronist government in the 1940s and 1950s was characterized by the expansion of social rights through employment – workers' conditions improved, and unions negotiated terms with the employers through state-sponsored coordination. The working class felt empowered politically and with the enfranchisement of women, who got the vote in 1949, there was real political progress. Perón was originally inspired by Mussolini, by the idea that instead of class war there could be coordination of class interests by the state. The unions strengthened by Perón won the loyalty of the working class. The economic elites hated Peronism for making the rural immigrants they called 'darkies' (*cabecitas negras*) feel themselves to be citizens with full rights. The left, including communists and socialists, were bitterly opposed to the Peronist project that offered cooperation with capital rather than revolution.

After Perón was deposed by a military coup in 1955, what remained of his legacy was the corporatist model of giving government the role of coordinating economic forces. In the subsequent period, this model was used as much by military dictatorships as by democratic governments. Civil and political rights were eclipsed by struggles for economic and social rights, until the last brutal dictatorship of 1976 brought them back into sharp focus. The death and disappearance of those with left-wing political views was the thorough negation of civil rights. From the extreme of having to defend basic human rights against the state, a new understanding of politics gathered force – and democracy is still held to be precious in Argentina.

By the 1970s, Argentina had lived through nearly 20 years of Peronists being forbidden to stand in elections. Although the military allowed short 'democratic' interludes, these ended in coups.[11] A new generation of

Peronists decided that if the working class was Peronist, they would have to take the revolution to them. This became the origin of a left-wing Peronism that saw idealistic young people join the armed struggle, as many others did across Latin America in pursuit of social justice and democracy. Many more reinvigorated the ranks of social organisations with the same ideals. Among these were law students Néstor and Cristina, in La Plata University, an hour south of Buenos Aires.

Their political coming of age coincided with the extreme political violence that saw the military and police kill or disappear approximately 30,000 people (there are no exact figures, as perpetrators have not released records). A generation of mainly young Peronist activists was decimated and the left-wing of the movement never regained the ascendancy within the Justicialist Party or in national politics. Until the Kirchners came to power.

This background marked the governments of the Kirchners, and the same social fault lines evident under Perón re-emerged during their mandates. Both Néstor and Cristina were first and foremost Peronists: but they were left-wing Peronists, combining the appeal to populism with an inclusive stance towards workers and the vulnerable. In the intervening decades, the Peronist unions had lost political weight: first to the concerted murders and disappearances of the last dictatorship (about a third of victims of state terror were trade unionists), and later to the privatizations and unemployment caused by neoliberal reforms, undertaken by a nominally Peronist president, Carlos Menem, in the 1990s. The national trade union confederation splintered in the 1990s into two CGTs (*Confederación General del Trabajo*) and a new one that emerged to their left, the *Central de Trabajadores de la Argentina* (CTA).[12]

Although Néstor Kirchner established good relationships with the union confederations, he also sought out other support in organised civil society. The most visible of these partnerships was with the *Madres of Plaza de Mayo*, and by extension with other human rights organizations. We look at how these links developed in the next chapter on Néstor Kirchner. It is worth a mention here because the Kirchners' strong affinity with 1970s politics brought to light the unresolved conflicts of that decade.

The human rights movement created a politics of memory that was built on universal human rights, but also on the lives of the overwhelming majority of victims: young progressive activists. Argentina has pioneered justice for crimes against humanity in court, but it has never carried out a truth and reconciliation process that recognised the extent of support across society for the coup and for military intervention. Trials have achieved partial justice, and the main way the military and their supporters resisted justice has been by withholding evidence and information.

Thus Kirchner's alignment with the Madres had greater consequences than perhaps he intended. On the one hand it gave state support to the recovery of evidence of human rights abuses and their due process in court. But it also politicized the human rights movement, bringing its organizations into party political strife and diminishing their moral standing. Conservative and apolitical sectors of society who believe that left-wing activists who were killed 'must have done something wrong' felt vindicated, equating human rights with left-wing demands to defend political interests. One catastrophic result of this association has been to embolden the right to actively undermine human rights work, now portrayed as sectarian. The polarization was deepened by the renewed emphasis on the ideological clashes of the 1970s. Since the return to democracy in 1984 there had been disputes in the public domain, with the right interpreting the human rights movement's call for justice as seeking revenge; while the left-wing imperative not to forget or forgive (*ni olvido ni perdón*) clashed with an unrepentant right-wing that felt they had saved the country from revolution. What little common ground had been achieved in establishing justice for the crimes of the dictatorship over 20 years was reduced. The controversies unleashed revealed how difficult it is in Argentina to imagine a justice system that does not depend on political power, and vice versa.

3. The rift

After 2008, common ground seemed to shrink in all areas of public life. When the governments of Néstor Kirchner and CFK felt under threat, they came out fighting, and promoted only unswerving loyalty. Criticism was construed as an attack, never as constructive; the opposition hurled personal abuse more often than policy proposals. Media outlets were identified as being 'for' or 'against' the government. Those who did not feel represented by the vocal supporters and opponents of the government became fewer and fewer in public life and joined the silent majority that eventually voted against the government in the November 2015 elections. The desire to put an end to this open political warfare was a strong motivation: many voted against the polarisation, against the escalating rhetorical violence but not necessarily against the policies of the decade.

The enumeration of winners and losers from the policies implemented by the Kirchners doesn't explain the level of aggression and passion that they unleashed. Economics were trumped by emotional reactions to their leadership. Although some of their followers were very loyal, the Kirchners did not create passionate support in the majority of society. Their emphasis on 'the people' and the national interest encouraged the support of a small but vocal section of the middle class, the progressive thinkers and activists of civil society. And those who benefited directly from their measures felt that they were on the right track, but were also swayed by the daily barrage of media attacks against the government.

So what was the reason for the language of confrontation and abuse that became the norm between the government and opposing sectors of the middle class and the media? Economically the middle class had gained most, with those in formal employment seeing their incomes increase above the rate of inflation, a privilege not available to the forty per cent of the work force paid informally. They enjoyed subsidized travel (paying in instalments in pesos for flights and holidays); they had subsidized services, benefitting as much as the poorer citizens who were the main target of cheaper water, electricity and gas. So the confrontation wasn't really about money in pockets.

Much of the anger focused on the accusations of corruption against government officials.[13] A number of high profile cases were investigated and slowly brought to justice, although other legal causes languished. The indignation aroused by politicians taking advantage of public office speaks of people wanting more transparent and accountable politics. Neither transparency nor accountability were well represented in the Kirchner governments. But the weakness of a strategy to make corruption the grounds for discrediting the Kirchners is that most of the political class is tainted by it. In 2015, while the Macri election campaign centred on accusations of corruption against government officials, Mauricio Macri himself stood accused in 215 open lawsuits, some involving the misuse of public funds during his time as mayor of Buenos Aires. The fact that corruption is endemic is not to disregard it or justify inaction. But accusations in campaigns and in the media were used as partisan political weapons. Newspapers ran stories that suited their politics, while few voices were raised to insist on an independent judiciary to tackle *all* charges of corruption regardless of political affiliation.

If a reliable judiciary fails to collect evidence and try politicians of all stripes, it is because of an historic inter-weaving of politics and the judiciary. Corruption is not just a problem of politicians, it is a recognisable social problem, where personal relationships are key in gen-erating the trust needed to do business. Argentina suf-fers from a widespread problem of a lack of institutional structures independent of political influence. Even the concept of a permanent civil service is poorly defined and therefore not upheld.

Too often what was taking place on the front pages of the newspapers or on TV and on the radio airwaves were show trials where both sides put their case with scant evidence, while the media itself was lacking in transparency and ethics. Instead of reporting on legal cases, the media conducts summary sentencing in the court of public opinion. The headlines, especially between 2008 and 2015, were full of strident stories denouncing government misconduct, and the (fewer) government-supported media extolling the benefits of their policies. The facts were always contested, and opinions and interpretations were paramount. Critics of the government became so irate that it was hard to credit their independence; government propaganda was easier to spot, but some of it was based on truth, and it was harder to assess what was fact and what was spin.

Considering CFK's thundering speeches, you might expect class war, with the poor resenting the rich. But that was not the case. The poor in Argentina consider themselves 'middle class', working hard to consume, to have a phone and motorbikes and holidays. They are devoted to education and want their children to become professionals. With a system of free state education from age three to university, hard work and determination can turn into social mobility. Upward mobility has historically been possible in Argentina, with rural immigrants, and then those from neighbouring countries, arriving with a few years of schooling and able to see their children graduate from university.

It was not evident until CFK's measures began to be dismantled by the incoming Macri government, quite how much had been possible for poorer workers. As politician González Fraga said in an interview in May 2016 '[they] made an average employee believe that their average salary could buy them mobiles, flat screen TVs, motorbikes and trips abroad – that wasn't normal.'[14] He argued that this wasn't sustainable. Yet it had been sustained for over a decade, so the economics were possible, in spite of sustained opposition by economic sectors with the power to sabotage policy. The comments sparked more than indignation over economic policy though – his slip revealed a widespread *sotto voce* belief among the wealthy elites in Argentina that it just wasn't right that poor people should aspire to all that.

Class conflict is often expressed more strongly by the upper middle class – they are openly disdainful of those less wealthy than themselves. If under Perón they objected to workers gaining rights, under the Kirchners they resented the new rights of domestic workers, of gays and lesbians and transsexuals. Of course, prejudice was not exclusive to the rich; working people were also suspicious of the social protection benefits they saw as handouts, supporting idleness, even though no benefit was sufficient to live on.

The differences between those who believed that CFK's government was doing some good and those who thought that it was damaging became personal, bitter and rancorous. Journalist Jorge Lanata famously coined the term *'la grieta'* (the rift or break) in 2013 to describe the growing divide in society between those who supported the government and those who were critical of it. He blamed the government for creating enemies, and indeed the Kirchners' version of populism did create enemies; but Lanata did not admit that it takes two to tango, that neither himself, nor the media at large took responsibility for the divisive coverage it put out. The rift became visible to all when Argentina voted to oust the continuity candidate in the 2015 elections and instead chose change, even though many admitted they did not like Macri.

When we try to assess who gained what from the three governments of Néstor Kirchner and Cristina Fernández de Kirchner, we find that most Argentinians gained economically, but the country as a whole became more divided and less able to unite around the task of nation building.

Notes

1   The possibility to travel abroad is a big concern for the middle class in Argentina. A combination of cheap credit (buying in fixed instalments in pesos with high inflation) and a special dollar rate for travel agencies made holidays overseas affordable for those with credit cards.

2   http://www.perfil.com/politica/franco-mauricio-y-una-trama-marcada-por-el-manejo-de-una-millonaria-fortuna-0417-0023.phtml

3   http://www.diariouno.com.ar/espectaculos/
lanata-hay-una-grieta-argentina-que-ha-separado-
amigos-hermanos-parejas-y-companeros-laburo-
20130806-n1789
4   http://www.conflictosmineros.net/contenidos/
2-argentina
5   https://societyandspace.com/reviews/reviews-archive/
javier-auyero-and-debora-alejandra-swistun-flammable-
environmental-suffering-in-an-argentine-shantytown-
reviewed-by-thomas-perreault/
6   https://www.dukeupress.edu/patients-of-the-state
7   http://www.lanacion.com.ar/1911478-un-gandhi-
de-la-politica-argentina
8   http://link.springer.com/article/10.1007/s12116-
008-9037-5
9   Accessed November 22 2015, http://www.lanacion.
com.ar/1847531-el-lenguaje-economico-segun-
Néstor-y-cristina
10   https://www.imf.org/external/pubs/ft/fandd/2016/06/
pdf/ostry.pdf
11   Argentina had two democratic presidents in between military dictatorships: Frondizi (1958-1962);
Illia (1963-1966).
12   https://es.wikipedia.org/wiki/Sindicatos_de_Argentina
13   See 'Argentina probes ties between ex-presidents, Mi-
ami real estate empire' for an example of investigative
journalism, as http://www.miamiherald.com/news/
business/real-estate-news/article90028812.html
14   http://www.clarin.com/politica/Gonzalez-Fraga-
empleado-celulares-exterior_0_1584441638.html

CHAPTER TWO
Néstor Kirchner (2003-2007): a new kind of Peronist

The way to power

Néstor Kirchner seemed to burst onto the national scene from nowhere in 2003. Santa Cruz, the province he governed in Patagonia could be described as the back of beyond. He came to power thanks to the outgoing interim president, Eduardo Duhalde. At the time Duhalde was the most powerful Peronist governor, and

Nestor Kirchner addressing Congress, March 2007
Presidencia de la Nación Argentina. Creative Commons Attribution 2.0 Generic

he was the one who took charge of Argentina after the financial meltdown of 2001. In his book, *Memories of the Fire*,[1] he recounts the critical 16 months during which he ruled, and which largely set the bases for Kirchner's subsequent government. Duhalde took on a country in default, with no international credibility, where people had lost all patience with politicians ('*Que se vayan todos!*' Out with them all! they shouted on demonstrations). Duhalde had no mandate at the polls. He inherited a country full of angry people and somehow succeeded in stopping the slide into chaos and violence. The feeling of many in 2002 was despair. A large part of the middle class had crashed into poverty, pensions lost their value, work was scarce and people were leaving the country in droves.

The twelve years of Kirchner governments has obscured the legacy of the 500 days that Duhalde was in power. Even if everyone hoped that in 2002 Argentina had reached rock bottom, nobody knew which way was up. Somehow, Duhalde's administration overcame the social turbulence and financial disruption. He devalued the peso so that those with debts in dollars had them converted into the same amount of pesos – so, for example, if you had a mortgage of 40,000 dollars, you suddenly owed 40,000 pesos, equal to one third of the original amount. But if you had savings in a bank, for every dollar in your bank account, you were given 1.4 pesos – this meant losing just over half the value of your savings. For savers and pensioners, it was disastrous. To put these figures into context, it is worth remembering that on a national level, fewer than a third[2] of the population had a bank account, so the devaluation affected the urban middle class most.

The 'asymmetrical' exchange as it became known benefited those with the largest debts in US dollars the most – including some of the largest businesses and landowners in the country, those with access to credit outside Argentina. And so the pain was not fairly distributed, but it did spark off a productive cycle between 2002 and 2007 that led to the highest economic growth ever seen. It was Duhalde who put the emphasis on the 'productive' economy, the real work of creating jobs. Away from the financial miracles expected by the pretence that the local currency had the same value as the dollar and the privatization of state assets that had taken centre stage in the 1990s, he set the scene for a more involved and developmental state. Duhalde resigned over the death of two protestors during one of the many demonstrations in 2002. Before stepping down, he set a date for elections and supported Néstor Kirchner in his campaign for the presidency.

Varieties of Peronism

Kirchner took office on May 25 2003, a national holiday in Argentina that commemorates the first efforts the country took towards independence from Spain in 1810. Kirchner's first hundred days revealed that he was a type of politician not seen before in the Casa Rosada (the seat of government): a left-wing Peronist. From its inception in the mid-1940s, Peronism has always relied on the power of workers and unions – and yet Peronism in power has tended to be a conservative force, happier to rule with powerful elites, including the union leadership. In the 1990s it was widely felt that Peronism had abandoned the working class, when Peronist President Carlos Menem brought in radical neo-liberal reforms that included the privatisation of all state assets, including pensions.

From the 1950s onwards, the unions that Juan Domingo Perón had helped to strengthen had become powerful hierarchical organisations where loyalty was paramount. Their influence was cemented by the nearly two decades of 'resistance' (1955-1973) – the period when Perón was forbidden to stand for election by military dictators, and the union confederation was the only legal vestige of 'Peronism' that could defend the social gains made by workers under Perón's governments (1946-1955).

By contrast, Kirchner hailed from a wing of Peronism that came to prominence in the 1970s, alongside left revolutionary movements throughout Latin America that advocated social justice, and took up arms to fight against military dictatorships. Kirchner was a political activist rather than a proponent of armed struggle and he avoided state repression; yet many of his generation were killed or were disappeared by the security forces. Among them were close friends and fellow students from his days at La Plata University.

When he was elected president, his public support for human rights organizations brought back into the public eye the historic struggle between progressive young people and the state in the 1970s, when the armed forces backed by the police and large sectors of the middle and upper classes used repression to destroy emancipatory politics. The language Kirchner used referred constantly to this defining moment in Argentinian politics. This was the political context in which he and his wife Cristina Fernández de Kirchner (CFK) cut their political teeth, and they were both aware of the calamitous defeat at that time of a project for progressive social change.

A reminder of the diversity within Peronism, as well as its pre-eminence as a political force, was clearly provided when Néstor Kirchner stood for the presidential elections in 2003 against two other Peronist candidates. One of them was Carlos Menem, twice president during the 1990s. To distinguish his own brand of Peronism,

Kirchner created a political party called *Frente para la Victoria* (FpV). The FpV endured as the 'Kirchnerist' vehicle for CFK's subsequent electoral victories, as well as for a majority of Peronist provincial governors.

A weak president

When he assumed the presidency in May 2003, Néstor Kirchner was considered a 'weak' president. He had narrowly lost the first round of voting to Carlos Menem, who withdrew from the run-off when polls showed he would lose by a large margin in the second round. That left Kirchner taking office with 22% of the votes cast. To bolster his ability to govern, he immediately reached out to social movements like the *Asociación Madres de Plaza de Mayo*, to the unions, to left-leaning intellectuals and activists. He kept his distance from the party structures of the *Partido Justicialista* (PJ) at first, even though he was invited to lead it soon after coming to power.

He spent the first two years in power talking up a crosscutting idea of political organization (what he called '*transversalismo*'), as a way of bringing together support for his mandate beyond party politics. It was a canny strategy in a country where politicians of all stripes had lost credibility. Similarly, once in office, Kirchner sought to build an independent power base away from his immediate predecessors, the Duhaldes: Eduardo, and his wife Chiche, who became a national deputy in 1997 and a senator for Buenos Aires province in 2005.

The historic opposition to Peronism, the Radicals (the political party *Unión Cívica Radical*, UCR), had imploded with the collapse of the government they led at the end of 2001. The image of the last Radical president Fernando de la Rua escaping from office in a helicopter in the midst of riots was firmly imprinted in the public mind. The *Frente por un País Solidario,* FREPASO, which had ruled with the Radicals, also disappeared. Many of them, originally left-leaning Peronists, were absorbed into the Kirchner administration. For some time, the main opposition leader was Elisa Carrió, an anti-corruption campaigner. It seemed that Peronism's mantle had spread across the political spectrum and overshadowed all other forces. It wasn't until 2005 that Mauricio Macri joined forces with two other right-wing parties to create the coalition that would become the PRO (*Propuesta Republicana*). In 2005 Macri became a national deputy, and in 2008 he won the contest to become mayor of Buenos Aires, one of the most powerful political posts in the country.

What Néstor Kirchner did next was to make a virtue out of novel political moves. He liked to employ surprise as a strategy for unveiling policy changes. In his first 100 days he retired a great number of senior military figures; he called for Congress to investigate members of the High Court who stood accused of rubber-stamping Menem's political decisions during the 1990s – three judges resigned, and another two were eventually removed for misconduct. Kirchner then instigated a more transparent method for electing High Court judges that reduced the influence of the executive in the process.

As well as this internal 'house cleaning', he set out to regain the world's lost confidence in Argentina after the 2002 economic default. He sent competent ministers and ambassadors onto the international stage and prioritized dialogue with the financial institutions that had a stake in Argentina's debt. Another surprising move in foreign relations was the way he reached out to Brazil; the often tense relationship between the two countries, based on mutual competition, became one of dialogue. Brazil remained the country's main trading partner, with over 20 per cent of exports and nearly 30 per cent of imports.[3] The surprise was in Kirchner's recognition of Argentina as supporting rather than competing with Brazil. The solid relationship built up with then President Lula (Luiz Inácio Lula da Silva) of the Workers' Party improved commercial relations, which were important for both countries, but also helped to shape an emerging regional power block with the capacity to propose alternatives to the foreign relation aims of the United States. This meant strengthening Mercosur, the never-consolidated trading union in the southern cone, and formulating an alternative to the ALCA (Área de Libre Comercio de las Américas), a free trade agreement proposed by the US in the 1990s that included all countries in the region except Cuba. Kirchner was active in the creation of UNASUR,[4] a union of South American countries established to act as a counterbalance.

Yet the foreign policy combat that gained him most recognition was with the International Monetary Fund (IMF). Negotiations began as soon as he came to power, but in early September 2003, Kirchner refused to use Argentina's reserves to pay a debt instalment to the Fund. As *The Economist* magazine put it, 'after missing a [US]$2.9 billion payment to the International Monetary Fund on September 9th, [Argentina] distinguished itself with the single largest non-payment of a loan in the Fund's history.' The IMF was pushing for its usual recipe of austerity measures and the reply was that austerity had taken Argentina to recession and disaster, so why make the same mistake again? Economist Mark Weisbrot saw the stand-off differently: 'Kirchner temporarily defaulted to the IMF rather than accept its conditions.[5] This was an extraordinarily gutsy move – no middle-income country had ever defaulted to the IMF.'

The tense confrontation ended when the IMF blinked first, rolling over the payment, and agreeing to take less. The Fund was also vocal in its advocacy of private interests, demanding rises in tariffs for public services, and was roundly told off for acting on behalf of big business. At the end of 2005, after increasingly hostile relations, Kirchner announced that Argentina would pay off the whole of the debt owed to the IMF, saving millions in interest. Politically it was a hugely popular decision. It bought Argentina financial independence from Fund demands, even though the reserves to pay it off had to be financially engineered into national debt in pesos.

Human rights

One of Néstor Kirchner's first actions in government was to send a project to Congress to annul the amnesty laws passed by president Raúl Alfonsín in 1986-87: *Punto Final (Full Stop)* and *Obediencia Debida (Due Obedience)*. These laws halted the trials against those accused of crimes against humanity; they were passed at a time when the military retained considerable power and threatened to disrupt the recently-restored democracy. While 280 cases were heard, a further 600 were prevented by the Full Stop Law, and most of those found guilty were subsequently pardoned by President Menem in 1989–90. In 1985, having regained democracy only in 1983, legal proceedings had begun against the military ex-heads of state in what became known as the 'Trial of the Juntas'. The trials found many senior military leaders guilty, and sentenced them to life imprisonment. Never before had a nation put on trial those politically responsible for mass human rights violations in their own country. It remains a hugely important precedent in the global work of human rights protection and has helped establish the possibility of redress against institutional violence across the world. One of the assistant prosecutors in the trials was Luis Moreno Ocampo, who went on to become the first head of the International Court of Justice in The Hague after its creation in 1998 to investigate crimes against humanity across the globe.

In peace processes in many countries there is often a trade off between truth and pardon; sometimes this exchanges a commitment to disclose the fate of victims for amnesty for the perpetrators of crimes. In Argentina this process never occurred, as the amnesties given were political projects designed to improve democratic stability. The apparatus of state repression was never exposed; aspects of it have only been revealed, painstakingly, by the forensic work of human rights organizations. Reconciliation does not form part of the language of human rights in Argentina. Instead, there is a sense of unfinished business, of a war that continues by other means as the military still refuse to provide information about the deaths of civilians they perpetrated, while the especially cruel crime of 'disappearance' offers relatives no body and no place to mourn. The search for truth became a crusade.

The attempt to bring closure to the disappearance of thousands of people impelled human rights organizations to make memory and the search for the truth their goals. The phrase 'Against injustice and impunity. No forgiveness, no forgetting' (¡Contra la *injusticia y la impunidad! Ni perdón ni olvido*), a Bertolt Brecht quote, became their rallying cry. Memory became a struggle against oblivion, the search for information a weapon against impunity.

Against a background of the pardons granted by President Carlos Menem in the 1990s, Kirchner met with the Mothers and the Grandmothers of Plaza de Mayo the day after coming to power. The *Madres* are emblematic even though they are only one of many human rights organizations. They were the first to have the courage to protest against the dictatorship in 1976, while the military were still in power, and they continued in spite of suffering violence themselves and indifference in the 1990s and served as the uncomfortable voice of the country's collective conscience.

That first meeting was to be the beginning of a warm, personal bond that Kirchner developed with Hebe de Bonafini, the leader of the *Madres*. Her astonishment at having found a leader receptive to her demands placed Kirchner squarely within progressive politics and the support of human rights organizations enhanced his moral standing with the nation. As she put it, 'he's not like all the others' which, coming on the heels of calls for a renewal of the political class - '¡*Que se vayan todos!* Out with them all!' – was high praise indeed. By putting himself on the side of the Madres, Kirchner also placed himself alongside the groups that had grown after the mid-1990s, organizing against neo-liberalism and the rise of poverty and unemployment in Argentina.

When Kirchner spoke to the UN General Assembly in September 2003, he said 'We are all sons and daughters of the Madres and Abuelas de la Plaza de Mayo'. After his death in 2008, Hebe wrote an open letter[6] claiming him as another of her children, saying how proud she was of his passion and his principles, and how happy she was that he had brought young people into politics. The Madres had arrived at the heart of political power, and stayed there until the end of Cristina's mandate in 2015.

To emphasize that he meant business over human rights, within a week of coming to power Kirchner retired the senior heads of the armed forces. A year later, on March 24 2004, during the events commemorating the 1976 coup, Kirchner made the chief of staff of the army take down the portraits of Jorge Videla and

Reynaldo Bignone, two de facto rulers of the juntas from the walls of the Casa Rosada, in a symbolic but deeply felt attack on the military. On the same day, the new leadership of the Navy was forced to hand over one of the best known clandestine camps set up to torture and kill political activists, the ESMA (*Escuela de Mecánica de la Armada*), for it to be turned into a space devoted to memory. Reclaiming this prominent building on a major avenue in Buenos Aires had been a demand voiced by human rights organizations for many years. During the governments of Kirchner and later CFK, the Espacio Memoria y Derechos Humanos became the hub for a reinvigorated human rights movement.

From strength to strength

Although interim president Eduardo Duhalde disappeared from view, Kirchner was happy to continue with most of his predecessor's economic measures, providing the country with a welcome sense of continuity after so much upheaval. By the time Kirchner took office, economic activity had begun to pick up. The 2002 devaluation had lowered wages significantly, and production accelerated in most sectors of the economy, while money kept abroad by Argentinians was brought back to invest in cheap real estate and to create new productive areas of the economy.

With the unwavering support of human rights organizations providing public proof that Kirchner's government was 'different' and that he really did care about the people, other organizations were open to his proposals for a new emphasis on the state's involvement in making the economy deliver social goods for ordinary people. Especially in the first years of his government, the president was recognized for refusing to use force against social protest, even when marches cut off traffic in the city of Buenos Aires and frustrated drivers swore loudly and the newspapers condemned his 'softness'.

Yet the main source of his growing strength came from the economy. Economic activity grew in leaps and bounds, and he made political capital from growth that averaged 8 per cent annually during his tenure. Employment grew, poverty fell, incomes increased, commodities brought in high profits and taxes, tax collection was improved and social protection programmes expanded. How was all this achieved?

The economy

In the first instance, Kirchner kept Duhalde's finance minister, Roberto Lavagna, in post until he was asked to step down in 2005 due to the president's wish to have more control over economic affairs. Some emergency measures designed to overcome the economic contraction of 2002 – capping charges for services, taxing commodity exports and bank transactions – were kept in place long after the emergency was over, quietly increasing the government's reserves. The devalued peso made materials and labour cheaper while increasing the cost of imports, so that from 2001 onwards Argentina began recording trade surpluses. The growth in demand for goods and services was mostly met internally, which in turn generated more jobs and investment.

The virtuous circle was completed by the government aiming to ensure that the economy served social needs directly, rather than waiting for benefits to 'trickle down'. The main contributions expected of private businesses were not especially onerous: to pay workers' social security as part of formal contracts and to pay taxes. Yet in a country where informality – that is, working without a contract that includes a pension or healthcare – was the norm for over half the working population, and where levels of tax evasion have historically been high, it meant trying to effect a profound change in the relationship between the state and the private sector.

One of the achievements of the decade was to increase state income from taxes to levels never seen before. The national tax base as a per centage of GDP in 2002 came to 19.9 per cent; by 2013 it had risen to 31.2 per cent, the second highest in the region and close to the OECD average.[7]

Argentina has historically relied on exports of raw materials. During the period up to 2008, the international price of commodities was high and exports grew to record levels. Argentina's main exports were cereals, fats and oils, beef and related products and dairy products (36 per cent of total exports); motor vehicles and parts (12 per cent); chemicals and related products (7 per cent); and crude oil and fuels (5 per cent).

This gave President Kirchner a solid base to build on, and he had ambitious plans for how the state could manage the economy. By all accounts he was not an easy president to work for, as he had strong opinions about economic policy and how it should be conducted; he was reported to be involved in policy design in all areas of the economy, from tax collection to industrial incentives. As with his political actions, in economic decisions he showed what writer Beatriz Sarlo called a mix of 'calculation and audacity'.[8] He was a strategic thinker who was able to negotiate pragmatically with any ally or enemy; and yet there were also times when he used surprise and sheer front to forge ahead.

As outlined above, one such symbolic gesture that used finances to secure the national interest involved

Argentina's debt to the IMF. In January 2005, Kirchner announced that Argentina would be paying off its debt to the IMF, in full.[9] And sure enough, the country handed over US$9,535 million to the Fund and shook off an influence that had weighed heavily on governments for two decades. It was a declaration of financial independence. At the time, left-wing critics argued that this payment was not a priority, when social conditions remained precarious; other critics argued that it was all for show, as the debt to the IMF was small compared to the total external debt, that it was a populist gambit to win support. The relationship with the IMF mattered because after the country defaulted on its foreign debts in 2001, no international financial institution would lend to or otherwise invest in Argentina. Only the IMF provided loans, with the condition that they be used to pay other creditors. Paying them off bought Kirchner breathing space to negotiate with other creditors. It was also a huge public relations coup inside Argentina. The IMF was held responsible for the economic 'advice', in fact binding conditions, which partly shaped the neoliberal agenda of the 1990s. The Fund had pushed for the privatizations which meant that Argentina lost control of key assets, such as oil. The subsequent privatisation of pensions sent the country's debt spiralling towards crisis in the late 1990s.

Kirchner was able to pay off the IMF in 2005 because his term in power coincided with the most dynamic five-year period that Latin American economies had seen in nearly a century.[10] In Argentina, annual economic growth surpassed 8 per cent every year between 2003 and 2008, a rate of growth it had not seen since the beginning of the 20th century. The economy slowed in 2009 due to the international financial crisis, but even so, the average annual growth between 2003 and 2013 was over 6 per cent.

In terms of Argentina's total external debt the money owed to the IMF was not a significant amount, but it did signal Kirchner's intent to meet the country's international obligations. However, he negotiated hard to pay debt on Argentina's terms and not the creditors'. He offered Argentina's private debt bondholders 25 per cent of the value of the original bonds, pointing to the devaluation Argentina had endured in the interim, and the still significant levels of poverty and unemployment in the country. Eventually, over 80 per cent of bondholders accepted the proffered 'haircut' and new bonds were issued. In the box on Vulture Funds below you can read about the ones who held out.

The emphasis on settling debts, expanding the tax base and investing in infrastructure created a virtuous circle for the growing economy. The missing component was incentives for investment, certainly for foreign observers nervous of the instability created by the currency crash of 2001. In practice, 'grey' money held by Argentinians abroad flowed in – land was bought, houses were built and changed hands (private construction grew at nearly 10 per cent annually between 2003 and 2010), new cars appeared on the roads and many areas of production were modernized with new machinery. Argentina might have been a pariah in international markets, but in practice money looking for a return became available, although it was often not clear where it came from.

The foreign companies that had bought up state assets in the 1990s were not happy to have restrictions on the profits they repatriated, as the Kirchner government put pressure to keep prices low, particularly for basic services. The struggles over the control of prices and eventually of services was to lead to a series of re-nationalizations.

Vulture Funds

With Argentina in turmoil in 2001, President Eduardo Duhalde and his economics team decided that a key tool in reducing the country's debt was to default on its interest payments on international public and private debt, amounting to some US$132 billion. They offered private investors holding Argentinian government bonds–in the main foreign banks and hedge funds–one third of the face value of the bonds, with the promise of a further payment when the Argentinian financial situation recovered. More than 90% of the bondholders reluctantly accepted this deal, and were paid some 30 per cent of the face value.

A remaining 7 per cent of bondholders held out against the offer, hoping they could claim a higher per centage through international courts. This is because the legal guarantees for the original bonds are signed in the world's financial capitals such as New York, London or Frankfurt, which have a legal framework to settle these kinds of disputes.

However, as they year went on many of those holding bonds were not the original investors. Instead, the bonds had been bought up at a large discount by companies that specialize in purchasing cheap debt and then work to force the defaulting government to pay by means of lawsuits. These are the 'vulture' funds, so called because they prey on the dead meat of international finance.

In the case of Argentina, the most aggressive of these vulture funds has been NML Capital. This is a subsidiary of Elliott Management, a hedge fund based in the United States. Since 2002 NML has taken the lead in pursuing the Argentinian authorities through federal courts based mainly in New York. NML and others went to great lengths to force the Kirchner governments to pay a larger per centage to redeem the bonds, including at one point attempting to seize an historic Argentinian training ship while it was on a goodwill trip to Ghana.

Finally, in a 2012 judgment that became effective in 2014, Judge Thomas Griesa of the United States District Court for the Southern District of New York ruled that Argentina must pay the vulture fund bond owners back at full value, at a cost to Argentina of US$4,65 billion.

At the same time, the judge barred Argentina from completing payment to the bondholders who had accepted the rescheduling of their debt until it had paid the vulture funds. Cristina Fernández de Kirchner called this blackmail, and in July 2015 Argentina technically defaulted a second time, refusing to comply with the US ruling.

One of the first moves by the Mauricio Macri government early in 2016 was to accept the US ruling. Macri argued this was the only way for Argentina to be able to return to the international financial markets and issue new bonds. Argentina has now paid the holdouts some US$4.65 billion. Of this, according to Nobel Economics prizewinner Joseph Stiglitz and the economist Martín Guzmán of Columbia University Business School, NML capital has received some US$2.3 billion for an investment in the region of US$177 million, a return of 1,180%. To add insult to injury, Argentina also paid the vulture funds' legal fees.

President Kirchner felt it was essential for the state to play a central role in planning the economy and having an overview of economic development. Additionally, he believed it was the state's responsibility at a time of economic necessity to lead the way in building infrastructure so that economic activity could be more socially useful. One of his most trusted ministers was Julio de Vido, in charge of the Ministry for Planning and Infrastructure, a ministry that grew as projects multiplied. Roads spread across the country, radiating from Buenos Aires. Airports were renovated, houses were built, schools refurbished. While the improvements never seemed sufficient to meet demand, slow progress was visible. A motorway joined Buenos Aires and Córdoba, the second largest city in the country. Ruta 14, once the most dangerous road in the country, became a dual-lane highway, with piecemeal improvements between 2004 and 2014 slowly connecting thousands of kilometres. It is the road used by lorries from Brazil and Paraguay, and connects Argentina to Uruguay via long bridges over the rivers Uruguay and Paraná.

The volume of investment and the lack of transparency in the process of tendering for large contracts raised suspicions that government officials could be personally benefitting from the projects being undertaken. Although administrative processes were in place within ministries, large economic decisions were taken on the basis of trust and loyalty. The power of networks and relationships has always been transcendent in Argentina, at all levels of economic and political activity.

One case where corruption has been proven was in the more familiar guise of private companies paying off public officials to loosen state oversight and provide subsidies. In 2012 a train crashed at one of Buenos Aires' main stations, causing the deaths of 52 people. It was discovered that the private company that had owned the trains since the 1990s had been paying for flights and apartments for Ricardo Jaime, the Transport Minister between 2003 and 2009. Along with senior company managers and his successor in office, he was sentenced to prison at the end of 2015.

In summary, Kirchner began his mandate content to let a highly competent finance minister decide what was in the economic interests of the country. Two years into his government, Kirchner was unhappy with Lavagna's independence and he was replaced by a more amenable and loyal minister. Economic growth was used to invest in tangible infrastructure and to boost social spending, particularly in education and poverty relief. The expansion of social protection not only reduced poverty, but fuelled consumption, becoming part of the dynamics of economic growth. Under Kirchner, large economic interests such as agribusiness and mining were able to operate freely as long as they contributed to state revenues. The many critical voices raised against the environmental damage and negative social effects of both industries were suppressed or sidelined, so that there was little publicity in the media about the devastating impact of soya growing or large-scale mining. The government's tacit support in return for economic benefits was one of the clearest signs of the pragmatism that characterized Kirchner.

The return of jobs

As soon as he took office, Kirchner's minister for Work, Carlos Tomada, called for collective bargaining to restart after a decade of no government mediation in wage negotiations. The historic labour confederation, the *Confederación General del Trabajo* (CGT), united in 2003 around the figure of Hugo Moyano, leader of the lorry drivers' union. Moyano provided a reliable counterpart for the government until 2008 and contributed to Kirchner's success in managing wage rises which were annual and improved the real value of wages. At the same time conflict with employers was minimized by setting a cap on increases. A side effect of the growth of employment and the expectation of wage improvements was to reduce the ranks of '*piqueteros*', the most vocal of the unemployed protestors who blocked roads to call attention to their plight from the late 1990s onwards.

The next indication that workers' rights were back on the agenda was the government's policy of re-instating the minimum wage, with annual increments. The value of the minimum wage went from US$70 in 2003 to US$310 by the end of Néstor Kirchner's mandate in 2007. By mid-2015, at the end of CFK's two terms, the minimum wage stood at just under US$600 per month, making it the highest in the region. The political commitment to protecting the lowest paid continued even when employment ceased to grow after 2008.

Another piece in the puzzle of reinvigorating rights for workers was the new labour law, passed in 2004. It replaced a law of 1999 whose passage through Congress was mired in corruption. Although the rise in unemployment and temporary contracts during the 1990s made job security a thing of the past, it was not the labour code that had changed, but the extent to which labour rights were upheld in law. Judges were able to interpret the law in favour of employers where previously employees had been pre-eminent. With the government implementing privatizations and other neo-liberal policies for making labour 'flexible' for employers, the political conditions were hostile to employment rights in the 1990s. The labour code itself was not changed as much as unions claimed during the 1990s; in fact in the late 1990s the IMF was still pressuring the de la Rua government to change the law to shrink employment protection permanently.

The contrast with Kirchner's stance was telling. In 2004 a new labour code was passed by Congress and from day one the political backing from government meant that rulings in labour tribunals once more became favourable to workers. There were two main instruments used by government to signal this change in political will: firstly the expansion of the inspection duties of the Ministry for Work, including the number of inspectors and secondly public awareness campaigns warning employers who took on workers informally, without paying social security, that they would be prosecuted and fined.

Social protection

Although economic conditions improved rapidly after 2003, the sheer number of those affected by unemployment and poverty in the five years prior to that meant that many people were not able to walk into a job and improve their standard of living overnight. Kirchner inherited the emergency social programme *Plan Jefes y Jefas* (Heads of Household) that Duhalde had rolled out in April 2002. The programme provided a small cash stipend in return for community work. Many of the early beneficiaries carried out their obligations in social organizations such as soup kitchens, or in services that local government could no longer provide, such as looking after parks or playgrounds.

The introduction of Plan Jefas (70 per cent of beneficiaries were later found to be female) by Eduardo Duhalde signalled the intention to tackle social problems. During the 1990s the market was supposed to take care of social problems, and failed to do so. The social programmes created then were very small and failed the majority of those who had lost regular work and income. By continuing Plan Jefas and then creating new programmes to support the poor and employed to gain work, training or credit, Kirchner expanded the resources of the state aimed at including the poor and those unable to work, helping them also to benefit from economic expansion and growth.

Plan Jefas was one of the first 'cash transfer' programmes in Latin America, and the world. Although the idea originated in the 1990s, when 'workfare' was designed to compensate for the loss of employment generated by structural adjustment, after 2002 it was extended to reach many more beneficiaries. As the numbers receiving cash transfers grew, the idea of welfare in Argentina was transformed. Until then welfare had meant social security built on an insurance model: you work, you pay into the system, and when you become unemployed you get help for two years, and when you retire you get a pension. Plan Jefas was the first large-scale programme to use a cash benefit to alleviate poverty regardless of past contributions. It was assumed to be an emergency measure that would be unnecessary as the economic situation improved. The fact that a large core of beneficiaries remained on the programme pointed to long-standing poverty that was harder to solve.

The idea of giving a cash benefit to the poor in this way was unfamiliar in Argentina. Even help or hand-outs from politicians looking for support had previously been in kind, in the currency of favours, food, or material objects. Ordinary people who didn't know anyone on the benefits were inclined to think that it was counter-productive, making people dependent on the state when they should have been active in trying to make ends meet. Yet the benefits never provided sufficient income to live on by themselves, and therefore could not lead to welfare dependency. Cash transfers became part of the survival strategies of the urban poor, who combined them with informal work when it was available, and often informal 'recycling', collecting rubbish and selling the metal, paper or plastic that had value.

For the creators of the programme at the Ministry of Work it made sense to tie in the benefit to the strongly felt national work ethic, what they called 'the culture of work'. Although they were aware of cash transfer programmes in Brazil and Mexico that targeted food security and children's development, they felt it was important in Argentina to relate it to the world of work. Policy-makers took from academics the idea of 'employer of last resort', and made the state a temporary employer until the economy could generate sufficient jobs. Yet in spite of their best efforts, Plan Jefas was more akin to a token income benefit. In the hope that people would slowly cease to claim it, the amount provided was never increased. However, in 2008, nearly two million families were still receiving the benefit.

The minister in charge of Social Development, Alicia Kirchner, was Néstor's sister. She had been responsible for the same portfolio when he was governor of Santa Cruz province. She served under both Kirchner and CFK, although the nature of social protection evolved and changed significantly under each president.

Under Néstor Kirchner, a plethora of more than 40 programmes for the unemployed included inspectors to check employers' compliance with social security, coordinated industrial relations, training, promoting social enterprise and income-replacement. The main thrust was to create the conditions for work to be 'formal', that is, with a contract that included social security, health and pension contributions. They called this process 'formalization', and it was closely related to the traditional activities of the Ministry of Work and its responsibility over industrial relations and social security administration. Income-replacement was principally carried out through Plan Jefas, and social enterprise was fostered through the programme *Plan Manos a la Obra*.

This led Argentina towards creating a social safety net, something no previous government had ever attempted. The effects were to reduce inequality, increase internal demand and drive economic growth.[11] They also added to the inflationary pressures of the decade but the government explicitly privileged employment and a wider distribution of disposable income over monetary policy.

The incidence of poverty at the end of 2015 was still significant, and many critics of the government have pointed to this as a failure of the Kirchner years. Yet set in the context of growing poverty and inequality in the richer economies, and also in relation to the advances made against poverty in other Latin American countries, there was considerable progress. According to the World Bank, the rise in income per capita based on independent measurements went from under US$9,000 in 2003 to a high point of US$17,000 in 2011.[12] The continued demand for goods and services also suggests that the social impact of increased income was significant.

New beginnings, old stories

Néstor Kirchner was in many ways a new kind of Peronist: the first president since Héctor Cámpora from the left of the movement, with a personal history touched by the violence and political confrontation of the 1970s. For human rights organizations he was an ally; for unions he was a serious interlocutor; for the private sector he was a pragmatist who allowed them to grow their businesses.

He made much of his alignment with human rights organisations, and in the process of seeking moral authority for his government, politicised social organizations. Many of them became involved in implementing social policy, and worked in partnership with government offices. Over time many community organizers were also employed by national and local government offices. Social organizations and individual staff and trustees became involved in research, policy and implementation of new government programmes, particularly those concerned with social protection and human rights. Even the Madres agreed to take on state grants to support house building through the Foundation. The dangers of handling money and objectives for the government became apparent when those appointed at the Madres' Foundation to run the housing programmes were accused of corruption and malfeasance.[13]

On the international stage he soon acquired a reputation of being tough but realistic and willing to pay debts, which was reassuring to markets. Politically, he busied himself repositioning Argentina in the world, bringing it closer to Latin America and moving away from the United States. With Brazil as the senior partner he worked to open up new markets, predominantly with China and South-East Asia, and aimed for more co-operation among South American nations. With twelve other countries he helped found UNASUR, an organization designed to empower the participating nations to create their own integration programme, rather than the one pursued by the United States. In 2010, Kirchner was designated UNASUR'S first General Secretary, although his death in October of that year cut short his appointment.

He changed the tenor of how Argentina thought of itself. He had a positive story to tell about the country's possibilities: economic growth, more employment, more government involvement in making the economy work well for everyone. People liked his forceful decisiveness, a trait which did put him squarely in the box of what Argentinians expect of a Peronist leader: effective pragmatism. For the first few years of his term in office, government departments were busy publishing websites and printed material detailing their successes. Press conferences by ministers and by the president himself were frequent. Kirchner liked to have facts at his fingertips and his micro-management of many aspects of government shone through in his detailed knowledge of policy implementation. Yet early in 2007, an election year, as economic growth began to slow, the flood of data from ministries slowed to a trickle. In January 2007, the consumer price index that measured inflation at the National Institute for Statistics (INDEC) was altered by new officials appointed by the executive, while technical staff were fired. It soon became apparent that a range of national statistics were far from transparent, and staff were being pressured or bullied into deviating from standard research protocols.

Manipulating the figures for inflation and poverty became indicative of an approach where only favourable news was welcome. In the same period both Chile and the USA introduced reforms to their national statitics that were feared to play down poverty figures, but in Argentina there was no pretence of 'improving' statistics, no technical review, no open debate about the best way to measure poverty or consumer prices. Instead, staff loyal to the powerful minister for Commerce, Guillermo Moreno, infamous for his aggressive relationship with business leaders, took over the statistics office. The way the INDEC was treated raised fears of wider trends that deepened during Néstor Kirchner's time in government and continued under CFK. One concern was the approach that privileged the power to coerce over institution building, and a preference for convenient shortcuts rather than seeking long-term solutions. Another concern was that although people are aware that politicians will always tell it in a way that suits them, the strategy of brazenly puting forward a highly disputed version of economic affairs and refuse any debate on its reliability meant that the government's account was increasingly questioned. It sowed the seeds of generalized distrust spilled that over into scepticism with the whole of administration. There was disagreement about the facts but no space to debate and reach agreements. The populist approach that Néstor Kirchner and then CFK developed of creating an enemy and blaming entrenched interests for hindering a progressive agenda deepened latent antagonisms.

Those who supported the government as a progressive and redistributive project and those who felt the benefits of social and economic measures found any positive opinion of government drew scepticism and derision. The result was increasingly polarized opinions instead of exchange and debate. Time and his death have made Néstor Kirchner's legacy less contentious than that of Cristina Fernández de Kirchner, who succeeded him. Yet in many fundamental ways, their tenure was a joint effort, and Néstor Kirchner's period in office set the scene for what was to come.

Notes

1   http://www.lsf.com.ar/libros/11/MEMORIAS-DEL-IN-CENDIO/

2   http://www.iprofesional.com/notas/204367-Slo-un-tercio-de-la-poblacin-tiene-una-cuenta-bancaria-y-menos-de-20-hace-pagos-electrnicos [sic. Correct URL contains these apparent errors]

3   Followed by China (7 per cent exports, 14 per cent of imports) and the United States (5 per cent of exports and 10 per cent of imports).

4   https://en.wikipedia.org/wiki/Union_of_South_American_Nations

5   https://www.theguardian.com/commentisfree/cifamerica/2010/oct/27/nestor-kirchner-argentina-imf

6   p. 18. Cetrángolo, Oscar, Juan Carlos Gómez Sabaíni and Dalmiro Morán (2015) *Argentina: reformas fiscales, crecimiento e inversión (2000-2014)*. Serie Macroeconomía del Desarrollo. CEPAL, Santiago de Chile.

7   Beatriz Sarlo, (2011) Kirchner 2003-2010. La audacia y el cálculo. Buenos Aires: Sudamericana.

8   http://pausa.com.ar/2016/01/a-10-anos-de-zafar-del-fmi-el-ironico-retorno-del-megacanje/

9   CEPAL (Comisión Económica para América Latina y el Caribe) (2009), *Panorama social de América Latina 2008* (LC/G.2402-P), Santiago. Publicación de las Naciones Unidas, Número de venta: S.08.II.G.89.

10 López-Calva, Luis F. and Nora Lustig (2010) 'Explaining the Decline in Inequality in Latin America: Technological Change, Educational Upgrading and Democracy'. Chapter 1 in *Declining Inequality in Latin America: A decade of Progress?* Brookings Institution Press and UNDP. http://blog-imfdirect.imf.org/2013/05/06/after-a-golden-decade-can-latin-america-keep-its-luster/)

11 These figures are adjusted for spending power, making them more accurate than standard per capita measurements. Accessed June 2016, http://www.tradingeconomics.com/argentina/gdp-per-capita-ppp

12 Gasulla, Luis. *El Negocio de los Derechos Humanos.* Buenos Aires, Sudamericana.

CHAPTER THREE

Cristina Fernández de Kirchner, CFK (2007-2015)
Advances and conflicts

The Kirchners were a team: a formidable political duo that worked closely together. They had few peers and decisions were taken around what was popularly known as a 'small table', with carefully-chosen advisers. When Néstor announced that he was not standing for re-election in 2007 and Cristina was standing

Cristina Fernández de Kirchner
Victor Bugge. Creative Commons Attribution 2.0 Generic

instead, there was little surprise and a promise of continuity. In the end, in spite of the popularity of Néstor and his government's policies, it was a hard-fought election. CFK won the election in the first round with 45 per cent of the vote, but the opposition was split and the next two candidates between them polled 40 per cent of the vote.[1]

The continuity of policies was assured by the number of the ministers she re-appointed from the previous mandate. Carlos Tomada remained in charge of the Ministry of Work; Néstor's sister Alicia Kirchner remained at the head of the Social Development Ministry; Julio de Vido remained in charge of infrastructure at the Ministry for National Planning. Yet although many of the same advisers remained and Néstor himself was still heavily involved in decisions, CFK marked a change of style in wielding power.

CFK's approach to establishing her position was to be bold and explicit about her opinions. She became known for long, improvised speeches made to the nation on state-controlled media, in which she set out her policies. International profiles tended to describe her as the 'wife of' President Néstor Kirchner, but they overlooked the fact that her political career went back as far as his; that she had been elected to both houses of Congress in the 1990s and that politics had been her life since her student days. She may have been voted into the presidency in 2007 to succeed her husband as part of a political couple, but her re-election in 2011, following his death, proved that the electorate responded to her leadership.

Her inaugural speech in 2007 contained two memorable narratives: the first was that she was the product of the free state education system. This took her from a working class family in La Plata to a law degree and on to the highest office in the land. She made pointed references to being the first woman elected to the highest political office in Argentina, and seemed to assume that she would meet more resistance to her authority. That was the second strand of her speech, that she would put all her effort into the job, particularly because 'everything will be harder for me because I'm a woman'. This last became the headline in the newspapers the following day. It was an acknowledgement that society was not used to women in authority and that her ability and her judgement would be more closely questioned than a man's. She clearly meant this as a challenge rather than a passive acknowledgement. She was comfortable highlighting her sex when she announced that she wanted to be known as 'la president*a*', which is grammatically unnecessary. At first the debate inspired by her title and who used 'la presidente' o 'la presidenta' provided a map of who supported and who opposed her. Yet over time she won that battle: she was increasingly only known as 'la presidenta'.

Her power base in 2007 was a solid one. Both Néstor and Cristina had worked hard between 2005 and 2008 to consolidate their position. They had working majorities in Congress; Néstor was now leading the Peronist party, the PJ, making best use of its local reach; provincial governors and local governments were aligned with their leadership; the unified trade union confederation was a partner in annual negotiations; social organizations felt listened to and human rights organizations continued to lend the highest moral standing to the government. The media was generally positive about policies carried out under Néstor's mandate and welcomed Cristina's as a continuation of efforts that had seen unparalleled economic growth, a reduction in debt for the first time in decades, and a widespread feeling of progress and optimism.

Taxing times

Néstor Kirchner had inherited emergency taxation measures from Duhalde, and retained them: a tax on all bank transactions, for example, and export taxes on the lucrative agribusiness products that constitute Argentina's main exports, such as soya. In parallel, the push to create jobs in the formal economy translated into more income from taxes and social security, thus expanding the tax base. In a country where tax evasion at all levels of society is taken for granted, the increase was unprecedented. The poor pay consumer taxes but are less likely to pay social security or tax from commercial transactions, as cash is the norm in their daily transactions; whereas the rich, and this includes much of the upper middle class, have perfected multiple ways to keep their money outside of Argentina.

In 2008, CFK's new economy minister proposed a sliding scale system of taxes on grain exports, including soya. This would increase the rate of tax from 33 to 44 per cent depending on international prices. In 2012 Argentina was the world's fifth largest producer of soya, yet accounted for half of all world exports. Not surprisingly, these exports constituted a large proportion of Argentina's revenues. Some economists went so far as to explain the success of Kirchner's administration as 'export-oriented populism', the first successful combination of boosting exports and investing the returns in the urban poor.[2] This was politically possible because the main export, soya, had no significant internal market. In the past, Argentina's main exports, wheat and beef, had also been consumed inside the country, so that international prices affected internal supply and set up a conflict between internal consumption prices and international profits.

CFK expected resistance to paying more tax from the producers, but the fact that she might encounter difficulties rarely stopped her from taking unpopular decisions. However, she was not expecting the drawn-out conflict that mobilized thousands of people in 2008 and led to the defeat of her proposals in Congress. In the process, the best selling newspaper in the country, *Clarín*, went from supporting the Kirchners to becoming their strongest and most vocal opposition. It was the beginning of an enmity that would grow in intensity and vitriol on both sides.

Clarín, the power of the word

Héctor Magnetto, the visible face of *Clarín* media holdings, is infamous for having told President Carlos Menem that his public office was only the second most important job in the land, or put in other words, he reminded everyone that, 'Governments come and go, but *Clarín* remains.' *Clarín* is powerful because it has the largest circulation of any paper in the country, but also because it is much more than that: it controls radio stations and TV channels, internet access and for decades it controlled newsreel production. The paper's front cover is only the tip of an enormous media iceberg.

Magnetto's relationship with the Kirchners went through two very different stages. Between 2003 and 2007, cordiality reigned. *Clarín's* front pages endorsed government actions and opinion pieces were broadly positive. Favour was a two way street; in 2005 Néstor Kirchner passed a decree giving the media group automatic renewal of licenses for TV, radio and cable. They were also the recipient of between 15 and 23 per cent of official advertising revenue from the government across different media. In 2007 Kirchner approved another decree allowing the *Clarín* group to become the largest provider of cable TV, with 58 per cent of viewers. The relationship was felt to be mutually useful.

But Magnetto's historic threat that 'no government can stand three negative *Clarín* covers' was always there in the background. During the 2008 rural lockout, *Clarín* began to be more critical of the government and the relationship began to sour. During CFK's first year in power they still received the greatest share of official publicity: over 50 million pesos. But after 2008 it

(*Continue*)

Clarín, the power of the word (*Continued*)

dropped to minimal amounts and CFK was less accommodating and more confrontational. In 2009, when disputes arose between the Argentinian Football Association and the cable companies, CFK took the opportunity to involve the state in televising football, known as *Futbol para Todos* (Football for Everyone), depriving the Clarín group of significant income. But the real battle ground was a new Media Law, passed in 2009 (see Box p.75) which aimed to democratize access to the media and was felt to be a significant threat to *Clarín's* hegemony.

Clarín's response was not half-hearted. They ran not three negative covers but over 80 during the campaign for CFK's re-election in 2011. Magnetto also brought together other powerful business leaders to unite against the government[3]. CFK proved Magnetto wrong, winning the election in the first round, with the largest proportion of the vote ever recorded, 54 per cent. The battle lines were drawn and Magnetto reverted to the long game – negative coverage of CFK and the government continued throughout her second term and became more strident as time went on.

For the first time since 2003 there were protests against the government on the streets. Landowners affected by the tax proceeded to organize a lockout - a producers' strike with road blockades that lasted four months. It was surprising that a sector that involved relatively few people – landholdings in Argentina are immense, and mainly worked with machinery, rather than people – could mobilize people in the cities. Many middle class protesters had no stake in agribusiness. What brought them out onto the streets? Their grievances revolved around the high-handed way in which the measure had been announced and a growing resentment at being told what was good for them. CFK's forceful insistence that she was right played into the hands of *Clarín* who portrayed her as authoritarian. The way of she communicated became a growing focus for discontent, immediately revealing how different reactions were to strong leadership from a woman.

The way the new taxes were communicated to the public was confrontational and the government's response to the protests showed no concern for explaining the redistributive potential of the proposal. One of the practical problems of the proposed legislation was that it lumped together large and small producers. CFK said she was aiming to tax the extraordinary profits being generated by high commodity prices for an agribusiness sector that worked as a financial market offering enormous returns. It was hard to disagree

Research by the magazine Tiempo Argentina showed that 80 per cent of the front-pages of the newspaper Clarín were hostile to Cristina Kirchner during her first government.
Screenshot taken from report published by Tiempo Argentino. https://www.scribd.com/doc/75702519/clarin-80

with that. Yet in her heated defence of the measure, CFK referred to the whole sector as one - the draft law also sought to restrict the export of beef and grains in order to maintain supplies for the internal market and keep

prices from rising, a measure affecting smaller producers. By lumping them together, the government ignited
the ire of smaller producers, who in turn mobilized
urban dwellers. Trying to create a measure for the whole
agricultural sector and attacking them as one for being
more concered with extraordinary profit rather than
paying taxes turned out to be the wrong political line
in the sand for the government. *Clarín's* newly critical
front pages calling CFK authoritarian also explained
some of the urban discontent.

A dividing line could be seen across society, which over
time became a gap and then an abyss, leaving no middle
ground. In 2013, a journalist who was critical of CFK's
government termed it *'la grieta'*, the break or crack, a split
in society that became ever deeper, while a silent majority watched it worsen.[4] Public debate became increasingly
polarized, lacking any nuance or measure. Those who
complained of the president's high-handedness were vocif-
erous in their personal attacks on her. The press, which
during Néstor Kirchner's tenure had been cautiously positive, at this point became part of the opposition.

CFK inherited Néstor Kirchner's 'us and them'
approach to politics, identifying the enemy as the
traditional economic interests in the country. Even
though soya profits were mediated by financial speculation and short-term investments, the owners of the
land remained a small landowning elite, little changed
since in a century. In Argentina land had been given in
large 'gifts' to those who cleared it of indigenous people
through military campaigns in the nineteenth century,
or otherwise provided political service. This concentra-
tion of land ownership was never reformed. In theory,
it should have been easy to convince the majority of
the population to tax a tiny, wealthy minority, so the
support the landowners were able to mobilize was an
early sign of the problems created by the language of

confrontation and measures designed with no public consultation and presented as a fait accompli.

The vote in Congress came after months of protests. Support and opposition to the project began to define the political landscape that would shape CFK's time in office. 'Resolution 125' as it was known, was finally defeated in Congress by one vote. The deciding vote against was cast last, by CFK's vice-president, a politician from the Unión Cívica Radical, Julio Cobos. It made for gripping TV, as the country's political fracture lines were revealed in real time. Cobos had been asked to be her vice president in a bid to garner the non-Peronist vote. When he said 'my vote is not positive' he delivered a shock. In a country were loyalty is paramount it made him a political pariah.

The defeat of Resolution 125, the enmity of the most lucrative economic sector, criticism in the media, and the mobilization of sectors of society rarely moved to protest on the streets, might have caused CFK to rethink both her policy aims and the way she sought to implement them. But if anything, the fierce opposition had the opposite effect. She became more convinced of the need to confront what she denounced as the oligarchic and unpatriotic leanings of the protestors. Organizations of political activists, like the youth-led *Cámpora*, which had loosely supported Kirchner's government, began to organize in earnest to support CFK. These dynamics marked her tenure. To her supporters, it was the only way to achieve social change: by taking on the major economic interests and landing a blow first. To many others, the way of using divisions in society to govern, by the show of force and surprise, came to taint even policies they agreed with.

The middle classes

The scope of protest marches in the city of Buenos Aires, full of well-to-do middle and upper class people, widened

Soya

Genetically modified soya was introduced in Argentina in 1996, with no public debate. In 2008, more than half of Argentina's arable land was planted with soya.[5] The rich topsoil of the *pampas* (flat prairies extending for thousands of kilometres) can sustain two harvests per year, relying on the temperate climate and rainfall, so that no irrigation is required. The natural bounty is not just exploited, it is also abused with an onslaught of chemicals. The majority of the beans planted are Monsanto's Roundup Ready (RR), a type of soya that has been genetically modified (GM) to be resistant to the Roundup herbicide – mainly glyphosate – which is also manufactured by Monsanto.

Glyphosate herbicides have had their use restricted in many countries and cities around the world.[6] In Argentina the damage they are causing to the lives and health of populations living near aerial fumigation is documented and growing, yet they continue to be used on a massive scale.[7] The World Health Organisation (WHO) stated in 2015 that there is evidence that glyphosate causes cancer and genetic mutation. In that year, 300 million litres of the herbicide were sprayed over GM soya, corn and cotton from aircraft, raining chemicals on an area far wider than the target fields.

The damage caused by soya is not only environmental. The profits to be made in soya farming have seen its production expand into millions of acres of land that previously produced grains and sustained cattle. Reduced food production has pushed up prices of staples inside the country. Worse still, there has been no planning or oversight into how soya growing has expanded to less fertile lands; deforestation has been carried out in order to put more land under soya. At the same time indigenous and other subsistence farmers on poor marginal soils have been pushed off their land by large soya interests that can call on the support of local politicians and security forces. Soya monoculture has created even larger landholdings, in a country where rural ownership has always been in the hands of the few.

Enrique Martínez, the director of the National Institute for Industrial Technology (2002-2011), has been outspoken in his criticism of how soya growing has become a speculative activity.[8]

The investments required to pay for the expensive inputs and machinery required, and the extraordinary profits generated by two annual harvests bring few long-term gains for the country and only enrich a handful of investors. Soya production is highly mechanised, employs very few people and is almost entirely extractive: it is not usually linked in any way with local industry to process and add value to the primary product. It is also a speculative financial activity which receives a large amount of financial investment from those seeking extraordinary profits. Land is generally not worked by its owners, but rented out to large firms that carry out the agricultural work almost entirely with machinery and chemical inputs. When commodity prices were high, as they were between 2005 and 2008, and again between 2011 and 2014, returns on investment in soya outperformed most investment funds.

Additionally, for local producers, commodities such as soya are sold on the international market in US dollars, and so the devaluation of the peso in 2002 made costs in pesos much cheaper, and the profits from earning in US dollars higher. The wealth of soya producers was displayed during the conflict with the government in 2008, when they were able to withhold their harvest from the market for months to avoid paying the proposed taxes. The collective reserves of capital at their disposal make soya producers a formidable economic force within Argentina.

beyond the issue of soya production. The protesters were re-creating a historic split in the Argentinian middle class, a social division further marked by the Kirchners' 'you're either for us or against us' rhetoric. In the 1940s and 50s, under Perón, the split seemed clearer: the working class supported Peronism, the middle and upper classes were staunchly against him. Back then the minority of left-wing middle class thinkers were firmly opposed to Peronism, which they saw as tending to fascism in contrast to their own socialist or communist leanings.

But by the twenty-first century, when the majority of Argentinians self-identify as middle class,[9] and the country regards being middle class as part of its national identity, social and political differences are not so clear-cut. The working class that supported Peronism has been fractured by the high unemployment of the 1990s, and the disappearance of industrial jobs with their large shop floors and day-to-day solidarity. Although the unions remained strong, and mostly Peronist, they became increasingly middle class, with teachers and public service workers making up significant numbers.

The unsuccessful Peronism of the 1970s, represented three decades later by the Kirchners, was the start of a fusion of elements of progressive middle class politics and Peronism. There were practical reasons for this, especially the way social security is structured in Argentina, where by definition unions represent formal workers, most of whom identify as part of the middle classes. The privileged 40 per cent of workers with social benefits as part of their employment contract mostly access health and other benefits through membership of a trade union and, although this is not 'compulsory', to most intents and purposes it is required. Beyond that, the middle class breaks down into a 'progressive' sector that supports equality and labour rights and, more recently, social protection for the poorest, and a more conservative sector that aligns itself with the upper class, and feels that government support for the workers and the poor is always a vote-buying exercise.

Peronism was born out of a corporatist view that all interests should be coordinated by the state, but in practice it never managed to build a national interest above the bitterly opposed interests of different sectors of society. One oddity of Argentinian history is that Peronism's choice of corporatism over class war meant that the working class and the poor are not defined by antagonism towards wealthier citizens; in a culture that aspires to be meritocratic and where social mobility through education has been real for a century, success is more often assumed to align with effort. Class hatred, or if that is too strong, disdain, or prejudice, has been more often the province of the wealthy middle and upper classes, who openly disparage the poor and workers. The worst epithets in Argentinian politics are racist, the *'cabecitas negras'* (darkies), the poor who became socially visible under Perón and Evita, a term coined by the paler, mostly European immigrants of Buenos Aires city to refer to the darker rural immigrants. That old contempt, brought vividly to life under Perón, resurfaced at the end of CFK's time in office when it was applied to highlight her humble origins. In CKF's case, the combination of working class parents, acquired wealth and power and being a woman brought out an explosive mix of prejudice. Yet as was made clear in her inaugural speech, she knew what to expect.

Women and power

President Cristina Fernández de Kirchner was re-elected in 2011 for a second term with the largest margin ever achieved in national elections in Argentina. In her cabinet, three women ministers also extended their mandates in Industry, Defence, and Social Development. Women held almost a third of political posts across national, provincial and municipal institutions. The head of the Central Bank was also a woman, Mercedes Marcó del Pont. Women had arrived to positions of power in Argentina. Yet did they make a difference to how it was wielded?

The question is usually posed in terms of women using power to improve women's equality. According to international measurements, Argentina compares well in relation to neighbouring and similarly developed countries. The UNDP puts the country's Gender Equality Index as the highest in Latin America (ranked 67 out of a total of 146 countries in the 2011 index), taking into account access to education, health, economic activity and political participation. And although in terms of political participation and educational attainment Argentina would be much higher up in the rankings, it is pulled down by health problems and unequal income. Unsafe (illegal) abortions are thought to account for 30 per cent of maternal deaths, affecting mostly poor women who seek to interrupt their pregnancies. In 2011, for the first time, a bill was brought to Congress to debate the legalization of abortion, but it was thrown out on a technicality. At the time, CFK went on the record to say that she was personally opposed to abortion, although deputies of her coalition were allowed to vote according to their own convictions.

Did women advance in assuming positions of authority under CFK? A new index developed by the Latin American Team on Gender Justice argues that in reality women rule in very few bastions of power. In their report Sexo y Poder (Sex and Power) they concluded that out of ten key posts in society, women only filled two. And that although in politics their share was 36 per cent, only 4 per cent held senior posts in business; in unions, only 5 per cent had women in leadership positions, and less than 8 per cent of media companies were led by women. These results would seem to point to women advancing on the political front while lagging behind in economic and social leadership roles. The high degree of involvement of women in politics is partly explained by the *Ley de Cupos*, a quota law passed in 1991 that required at least a third of any electoral list to be made up of women. The law has been continuously in force for over 20 years, but the effect of having women in politics is yet to be felt in other fields.

CFK used International Women's Day (8th March) as a moment to make announcements dedicated to women, past and present. In 2009, she established the *Salón de las Mujeres* (The Women's Room), in the Presidential Palace, hung with portraits of an eclectic choice of notable women. In 2010 she used the occasion to propose improvements to the labour rights of domestic workers; the law she presented abolished the term 'domestic workers' as derogatory, and replaced it with 'personnel in private homes'.

Yet aside from these events on Women's Day, after that first speech she did not make much of her gender. She led forcefully, taking centre stage with speeches and actions. The press portrayed her as unable to control her husband's incessant political activity; yet their political partnership had never been in doubt and no disagreements were aired that suggested internal discord. At the same time as the media, and many political commentators, felt that Néstor had 'too much power', they also accused Cristina of being authoritarian in her use of executive power and frequent hectoring speeches. In sum, there was no evidence that she wasn't in charge, only that she relied on her husband as one of a select few who advised her and acted on her behalf, a role she had fulfilled for him during his term in office.

The death of her husband in October 2010 put an end to the speculation, as she stood alone at the head of the coffin for a whole day at the public lying in state. She told the press then 'not to confuse my pain with weakness', and an image of strength and unshakeable determination were born. People wishing her well wished her 'strength' and six months later, as she approached elections for her second term, 'strength' became the buzzword of her campaign. The billboards that said only 'Fuerza Cristina' played on the double meaning of being wished strength by the people, and the strength she projected. A further play on words in posters identified Cristina with varieties of power, 'la fuerza del amor' (the power of love), 'la fuerza del trabajo (the power of work), 'la fuerza de El' (His power [meaning Néstor]).

She constructed her power with explicit reference to her gender, and yet it is not in the feminist mould. Forbes places her in 16th place among the most powerful women in the world in 2012, yet she was in rigorous mourning for over two years after Néstor died. Unrelieved black is a social norm last observed by nineteenth-century Italian immigrants, not one common in present-day Argentina. Her dress code has gone unremarked. Her usual close attention to make-up and appearance has been a trait that foreign observers have interpreted as frivolous. But within Argentina, care of the self, and beauty, are not taken so lightly. Instead, they are seen as forms of what sociologist Catherine Hakim calls 'erotic capital', a key resource of the powerful, more easily manufactured than charisma, but similar in its effects.

Encouraging ways to be loved as a political figure, as well as feared and respected, has been part of the political culture in Argentina for longer than women's participation. The culture of power built up by men relies heavily on feelings of loyalty and relationships developed over time, rather than abstract values. There is also no evidence that the large proportion of women in legislative and executive power is changing the way in which power is exercised. The nature of power in Argentina remains vertical (instructions come from above) and executive (a very limited number of people make decisions). The political culture is based on striking decisions and actions, which require orders from a few, and obedience from many. In spite of the difficulties she may have faced imposing her authority, it is a model of power that was expertly wielded by CFK.

'The Model' reloaded

Néstor Kirchner began to describe his economic policies as 'The Model' early in his mandate, but it was CFK who made the phrase common usage – even if it came to public notice because her enemies disparaged it. The Model was a vision of the economy as serving social needs, with the state ensuring that the population's needs were delivered by both economic and state actions. It accepts capitalism as the means to organize economic activity, and is comfortable with the market having its own domain, but opposes the idea of a 'free market' – that is, the idea that the market is beyond political control, or that market rules should be applied to social life.

The idea of a developmental state, that is, a government that oversees economic activity for the benefit of society, has a long history, and opinion polls suggest that a majority of the population still support it, even after CFK has left power. The market is understood to be embedded in society, with reciprocal responsibilities. If the state guarantees the rule of law and infrastructure, for example, the expectation is that the market will contribute to social welfare through the payment of tax and social security. This is not socialism, as there is no ultimate aim to plan and direct the entire economy from government, and it does not stress the conflict of interests between workers and capital, but seeks to make the state the active 'co-ordinator' or arbiter of those differences.

The best example of this co-ordination was Kirchner's re-activation of collective bargaining, the annual meeting between the main union confederations representing workers and employers' organizations, mediated by government. These meetings agreed the range of wage increases for the year, and during CFK's two governments these negotiations kept wages for formal workers at least in line with the rising inflation, if not above it, gradually increasing the workers' share of national income.

Employment policies, supporting unions, expanding the tax base, extending social programmes: all these policies enjoyed widespread public support while the economy was growing strongly. Wages rose and the cost of living remained low due to government subsidies to public transport and utilities such as gas and electricity.

After the international financial crisis of 2008, economic growth slowed significantly and the government had less income to distribute. The uncertain conditions could have led to fewer demands on economic actors to deliver social goods, but the reverse was the case.

Some strategic companies privatized during the 1990s were renationalized by Néstor Kirchner, for example Aguas Argentinas, taken back into state hands in 2006, following disputes over the quality of the service. In 2008 it was the turn of Aerolíneas Argentinas, the national airline, as it headed towards bankruptcy; and in the same year the pension system was renationalized. In 2012 the state took over 51 per cent of the shares of the oil company YPF (*Yacimientos Petrolíferos Fiscales*), previously mainly owned by the Spanish oil company Repsol. In all cases market prices were paid for the shares and none of the private companies was expropriated.

The 2008 international financial crisis made the balance of trade less favourable and CKF's governments restricted imports and tried to force importers to export an equivalent value, leading car manufacturers to dabble in wine exports, and other forced exchanges.[10] The restrictions on imports were most visible in consumer goods, but their less visible impact was to create difficulties in importing capital goods and parts and accessories required by manufacturers and service industries. These accounted for 40 per cent of imports (closer to 55 per cent if fuels and lubricants are included). This meant that half of all imports were required for production, not consumption, and restrictions on them had a negative impact on the whole economy.

The Model that Kirchner had pursued, of economic activity delivering social goods, had to be revised in the light of international problems that affected the domestic economy. CFK decided to prioritize social spending and protection even before it was clear how to pay for it into the future. The changes in provision she introduced in 2009 were a fundamental departure from the welfare system that had been built up through employment. They extended to the most vulnerable, to older people and children, and reached well beyond the labour market.

Inclusion: social protection after 2009

From their inception in the late 1990s, the emphasis in welfare programmes in the late 1990s had been the 'culture of work': how to strengthen it, how to get people back into the labour market. Argentina had no history of benefits beyond those earned through social security payments in employment. Permanent employment was everyone's ideal – in Argentina it is known as the 'dependent relationship' (*relación de dependencia*), where in return for labour a worker can expect not only pay, but also protection from dismissal, contributions from the employer to the social security system, including health and pension funds. This is known as 'formal' employment and in most cases includes automatic membership of a union; this translates into pay rises agreed in collective bargaining at the level of union federations.

It is a system that works well for the 40 per cent of workers who are formal employees. Unsurprisingly, there are more formal workers the higher up one looks in companies, and among those with more education and better qualifications. The increase in open unemployment in the 1990s led to the creation of small workfare programmes where in return for work or training the unemployed received a small stipend. That system was expanded with the Plan Jefes y Jefas. Between 2003 and 2009, a variety of schemes were brought in to help, above all, men into employment, while supporting women to become carers, as another way of reducing the number of those seeking employment.

Government efforts also went into making self-employment in cooperative groups a viable option for workers left out of the labour market. Although the number of people was smaller than those reached by other programmes, the institutions that were expanded to support them combined the aims of generating employment, fostering cooperative development and community development. The main programme paid workers to build houses and urban infrastructure and in its final incarnation was called *Argentina Trabaja*.

Huge numbers of jobs were created, and poverty decreased with them. Yet by 2008 it was clear that existing welfare programmes were not improving the employment chances of the poorest workers, often working in sectors where formal employment had never been the norm, such as rural and domestic workers. In 2011 a new labour code for rural workers was passed that provided the same rights as for other workers. The same year saw a law sent to Congress to give domestic workers full employment rights, including maternity leave, paid holidays and a cap on the number of hours worked per week.. It was not finally approved until 2013.

Changing the rules of the game for employment was welcome, but relatively unfettered freedom for the market to decide on activity and investment meant that for many these rights were more theoretical than real. It did give workers the basis to demand better conditions, but fear of unemployment kept many working informally. The law and state enforcement were in favour of workers, a first step towards changing the culture of avoiding taxes and employers' contributions. The Kirchner government's efforts to bring more people into employment with social security were successful to some extent during the period 2003-2008, but began to stall after that. By 2009, 40 per cent of workers remained in the informal sector and beyond the reach of social protection.

The best evidence for the real, immediate benefits of social protection measures was seen for those *not* in the labour market. In 2004, a law of 'Inclusive Pensions' (*Plan de Inclusión Previsional*) extended the minimum state pension to those who did not previously qualify; this included self-employed workers, those without the requisite number of years in employment, and housewives. The new 'non-contributive' pensions as they were known, lifted a large number of households out of poverty. These minimum pensions were effective because they were regularly increased, not just keeping up with inflation in pesos, but slowly increasing their value over time. When Néstor Kirchner came to power, the minimum pension was 150 pesos (US$53), and by the time he left power in 2007, it provided 596 pesos (US$190);

under CFK the increases continued in pesos, so that by 2013 it was worth 2,165 pesos, although the value in US dollars did not increase significantly.[11]

For those too young to work, a radical re-design of social protection was introduced in 2009: a universal child benefit was made available to all informal workers, the unemployed and domestic workers. At a stroke, the mainstay of state benefits shifted from targeted programmes with significant outlay in terms of staff and bureaucracy to a universal child benefit centrally managed by the national social security administration (ANSES). Unlike previous welfare programmes where the monetary value of benefits tended not to increase with inflation, in a bid to discourage welfare beneficiaries, the Universal Child Benefit (*Asignación Universal por Hijo, AUH*) was indexed at regular intervals, in the same way as a long-standing child benefit available to formal employees as part of their social security package. The increases were ordered by decree until 2015, when they were made into law[12].

The expansion of non-contributory pensions to all older citizens and housewives, plus a universal child benefit, effectively created the first comprehensive safety net Argentina had ever known. Welfare was transformed from a pay-as-you-go scheme to one in which citizens have a right to welfare even before or after they have contributed to the labour market. The idea of inclusion was taken much further than any previous government had attempted. These new benefits were not opposed and suggest that they will endure beyond the governments that originated them. But it is an open question whether the length of time they have existed has been sufficient for them to be considered a right.

Identity and social inclusion

Economic inclusion was the first priority of CFK's administration, but she also made explicit efforts to use her visibility to bolster women's rights.. Women's rights to equality are enshrined in law in Argentina, but on a number of outstanding issues the reality is violently at odds with legislation. In terms of reproductive rights, the Kirchner and CFK governments advanced in tiny steps, as far from the limelight (and the influence of the Catholic Church) as possible, making contraceptives freely available and expanding sex education. The power of the Catholic Church to intervene behind the scenes meant that contraceptives rotted in warehouses and doctors were pressured to refuse to treat the few women who are entitled by law to have an abortion, such as victims of rape.

The other major challenge for women is male violence, present at all levels of society and leading to many, mostly undocumented cases of injury and death. Protest erupted in June 2015, organized by a diverse group of women from the media and social organizations, who called the first national march to raise the profile of femicide in Argentina. The march was called #NiUnaMenos, not one fewer, demanding that no more women should die at the hands of men, often in a domestic context. The Supreme Court and the government agreed to set up a registry of femicides and to create better records to support women suffering violence.

The mainstream support generated for the march was in part the result of an expanding sense of social inclusion. Women suffering or threatened by violence went from being caught in a 'private' drama to one where action was expected of government. During CFK's time in power there was a broad legal recognition of the rights to gender and sexual identity, and freedom to make a public commitment to identities other than conventional heterosexuality. These were a departure for a socially conservative society where the Catholic Church wields significant influence, both in the corridors of power and in the delivery of social services and education.

The new legal rights acquired by gay, lesbian and transsexual women and men were capped by a law that introduced marriage rights for gay couples equal to those enjoyed by straight ones. It was passed in 2010, and was in many ways in advance of society's openness to gay relationships; for many, it was the law that brought about a more widespread acceptance of homosexuality.[13] Coming out is still not an easy process, with widespread prejudice a common response. Catholic organizations were ready to protest and contest the legal advances, as was seen in the city of Buenos Aires: since 2002 the city's legal code has included provision for a civil union that could be entered upon by people of the same sex, but it was legally challenged by Catholic lawyers and not put into practice. Since the national law was approved in 2010, over 10,000 same sex marriages have been celebrated. The right to gender identity that became law in May 2012 included the right to choose how to identify oneself in legal documents, as well as state protection for the chosen development of gender identity. The law was hailed internationally for relying on the request of the interested party, with no 'expert' support required.

New political actors

In a world where politicians struggle to engage voters in general and young people in particular, the Kirchners succeeded in getting many young people involved in politics as well as many of all ages who perhaps had never felt that politics was relevant to their lives. On CFK's last day in power, in December 2015, something happened that had never been seen before: people turned up to Plaza de Mayo, spontaneously, not organized by activists, to wish her well and thank her.[14] They were women who had received housewives' pensions, gay activists who had married, transsexuals who had official documents in their chosen gender, domestic workers who had their work recognized alongside all other employees, young people who had come of age thinking that social protection was part of the national interest. No other president in Argentina has had a farewell gathering of this kind.

Young people in particular become politically organized under the Kirchners and were actively given a platform by CFK. The youth organization that came to prominence as a pillar of both their governments was the *Cámpora*. Founded in 2006 and named after the president elected in 1973 to enable the return of Perón to Argentina, it showed how vital the connection was for the Kirchners to their own political initiation, as youthful left-wing Peronists in the 1970s. The tagline on the Cámpora website, 'organization defeats time' also brings to mind the idea that they are reborn from the ashes of the historic defeat of the last dictatorship of 1976. The organization is led by Máximo Kirchner, son of both presidents, and was founded by a group of young activists who rose to hold considerable power under CFK.

Their original motto was 'our country is the other' and alludes to the role of social inclusion and transformation that they see as the purpose of politics. In the 2015 elections the Cámpora gained 24 deputies in Congress (out of 257) and three senators (out of 72). They appear to be more loyal to the Kirchnerist project than the wider Peronist movement in Congress, which has been splintering and voting with the Macri government instead of uniting as opposition.

Freedom of expression

A strange phenomenon grew during the time that the Kirchners were in power. People became more passionate about being in favour or against the government while 'moderate' debate and shades of grey lost ground in the media, and eventually, even in social situations. Those who disagreed with the government expressed their opinions stridently in books, and on social media. Those who supported them had to be equally clear and forceful.

A New Media Law

In any modern democracy, the media plays a central role in the quality of debate and access to information for the majority. In Argentina, media ownership is very concentrated in the hands of a small number of people. The law that regulated the media until 2009 had been passed in 1980, during the last dictatorship, and although there had been consensus across the political spectrum about the need to replace it, the political power of media companies stymied reform after the return to democracy in 1983.

In 2009, Argentina passed a new media law. The new law had been drafted by a broad coalition of community and social organizations in a process that included a broad debate across the country from 2004. This grassroots deliberation was not initiated by the government, although it was adopted after the Kirchners fell out with the largest media conglomerate which owns the daily *Clarín*, among many other outlets.

When assessing the law in 2009, the UN Rapporteur for Freedom of Expression and Opinion, Guatemalan lawyer Frank La Rue expressed that 'it is a model for the whole continent and for other regions of the world', as he felt that it was at the forefront of democratizing access to the media.[15]

One of Mauricio Macri's first actions after taking power was to use armed police to evict the workers of the Media Regulator office and thereby suspend the new Media Law of 2009 by force.

The different media outlets both fostered and reflected the polarization of society, although inevitably they were more often a reflection of their advertizers and sponsors and therefore the chorus against the government was much louder than the community media that supported government action. Diverse and nuanced opinions got little airtime anywhere.

There was critical scrutiny of the way government spent advertising revenue, supporting specific publications, which were then tainted as 'official' media outlets. Those opposing the government attacked the extensive use CFK made of the state media to speak to the nation on TV and radio.

The net result was a plurality of opinion and voices. It was not debate, and it certainly was not constructive, but it allowed for radically differing views to appear in the public domain. As we see in more detail in the Afterword, the plurality of opinion is notable in comparison with the uniformity of media coverage and recourse to police violence that has been in evidence during Macri's first few months in government.

A decade won?

On May 25 2013, ten years after Néstor Kirchner came to power, CFK spoke to hundreds of thousands of supporters, in a speech that became famous for claiming a 'decade won by the people'. The contrast was with the notion of a 'lost decade', originally used to refer to the effects of debt on social development in Latin America during the 1980s'. It became one of the most contested political slogans of the Kirchner years.

What did CFK mean by a 'decade won'? She was comparing the social and economic gains made since 2003 to the losses sustained during the 1990s, when neoliberal restructuring of the economy had provided temporary economic stability (1992-2000) at the expense of rising unemployment and poverty, and a loss of economic sovereignty due to privatization and newly spiralling debt.

In the last two years of her mandate, up to 2015, these claims were hard to defend. Inflation was high, imports were controlled and the vulture funds won the legal case to be repaid in full, putting at risk debt repayments, the agreements made with other debtors, and the country's reserves. Reports of corruption in her government came to light more frequently, and the unresolved death of federal prosecutor Alberto Nisman hung over her.[16] Her approach continued to be to make decisions with a small group of advisers, which were communicated in long speeches, without any attempt at dialogue with her detractors.

It was the most blinkered of her supporters and her enemies who dominated the media while a growing silent majority looked on as the Model seemed to have exhausted itself. CFK's chosen successor, Daniel Scioli, the Peronist governor of Buenos Aires province, was only tepidly endorsed. This might have been an electoral tactic, to allow him to emerge from under the shadow of 12 years of Kirchnerist rule, but he failed to provide a sufficiently clear or appealing alternative. During 2015 the opposition finally united and in November narrowly defeated Scioli in the presidential elections. 'Kirchnernism' was out of power.

And even though nearly half of the population voted for Scioli, in the immediate aftermath of the election it felt as though CFK was a spent power, and the slogan of the winning right-wing PRO, '*Cambiemos*', 'Let's change' really did capture the public mood. Something different was needed. However, although Macri never hid the nature of his pro-market, pro-US project the speedy and radical measures in favour of capital have continued to divide the country. Many of the achievements of the long Kirchner decade only became apparent when Macri took them apart. He sacked workers, meeting their protests with rubber and real bullets; he removed subsidies on services in the space of a few weeks, increasing the cost of water, electricity, gas and transport; he freed the currency market, devaluing the peso; he reduced taxes on exports, which substantially reduced state revenue; he took out international loans that have burdened the country with debt that will take decades to pay; he shut down by force the independent media regulator set up to oversee the new Media Law.

For the majority of Argentinians, the most tangible change since Mauricio Macri came to power is that life is hugely more expensive. Inflation has not been reduced, and jobs are at risk in a recessionary economy where the only ones turning a profit are large exporters.[17]

It is human nature to not appreciate what we have until it is gone. And yet wanting something better does not equate with rolling back the election decision and having the Kirchnerist Model back (although arguably Scioli would have also made significant changes). Argentina is locked into a political paradox that is older than CFK or Macri: people vote for strong leaders and clear projects, and then feel frustrated when the leadership does not rule by consensus and dialogue but instead imposes its vision regardless. In that context, there are always winners and losers, those who feel represented, and those who feel left out of the national project. Under Macri the winners are the media conglomerates, the exporters, the military, vulture funds. Under Kirchner and CFK the winners were the people who came out say goodbye to her on December 10 2015: the pensioners and the students, informal workers, the mothers and young people who felt that politics included them and that the country belonged to ordinary people too.

And yet that inclusion was built on confrontation and division. CFK failed to find a sustainable long-term economic and power base to sustain it. An inclusive economy that benefited the poorest was partly sabotaged by powerful economic interests that strained under state regulation; but it was also undermined by political leadership that told people to organize for their rights, but failed to create the open, diverse and solid institutions that would have enabled them to come together and demand those rights.

Notes

1   https://es.wikipedia.org/wiki/Elecciones_presiden-ciales_de_Argentina_de_2007

2   *Richardson, Neal P. (2009),* "Export-Oriented Populism: Commodities and Coalitions in Argentina", *Studies in Comparative International Development (SCID), Volume 44, Number 3.*

3   http://www.lapoliticaonline.com/nota/46010/

4   ¿El final de la grieta argentina? http://internacional.elpais.com/internacional/2015/10/24/actualidad/1445703385_149986.html

5   http://www.ecoportal.net/Temas-Especiales/Desarrollo-Sustentable/Republica_Argentina_impacto_social_ambiental_y_productivo_de_la_expansion_sojera

6   See for a report dated December 2015 and updates, http://www.pan-uk.org/search?searchword=glyphosate

7   http://www.lavaca.org/notas/confirmado-la-oms-ratifico-que-el-glifosato-de-las-fumigaciones-puede-provocar-cancer/

8   *Saber Cómo,* (Editorial) July 2008 http://www.inti.gov.ar/sabercomo/sc66/inti1.php

9   Adamovsky, Ezequiel. Historia de la Clase Media Argentina. http://www.planetadelibros.com.ar/historia-de-la-clase-media-argentina-libro-197641.html

10   http://www.bloomberg.com/news/articles/2011-11-02/porsche-sells-malbec-to-keep-autos-coming-into-argentina-cars

11   The conversion into US$ at the official rate did show an increase, but not at the black market value, making it difficult to convert the figures reliably.

12   http://chequeado.com/el-explicador/la-evolucion-de-la-auh-desde-que-se-implemento/?utm_content=bufferc293b&utm_medium=social&utm_source=twitter.com&utm_campaign=buffer

13   *La Nación*, July 2015. http://www.lanacion.com.ar/1810125-a-5-anos-de-la-ley-de-matrimonio-igualitario-casi-10000-parejas-se-casaron-que-cambio-en-la-familia-argentina

14   http://www.lavaca.org/notas/parte-1-plaza-de-mayo-9d-el-ultimo-acto/

15   http://www.pagina12.com.ar/diario/elpais/1-205669-2012-10-16.html

16   http://www.newyorker.com/magazine/2015/07/20/death-of-a-prosecutor

17   http://www.perfil.com/politica/Economia-argentina-Recesion-o-crecimiento-20160509-0010.html

CHAPTER FOUR
Afterword: End of an era

In early October 2015 presidential candidate Mauricio Macri unveiled an outsized statue of Juan Domingo Perón in Buenos Aires. Macri, a wealthy, privately educated businessman who has tended to look outside the country's borders for policy inspiration, embodies everything and everybody that has opposed Peronism. Given Perón's towering presence in Argentinian politics, one might expect many statues of him to be scattered throughout the city. But he is also a controversial figure, and so this was, in fact, the first in his honour. Another statue has been in the offing for years, under the auspices of the national government and Perón's own Justicialist Party, but it has never quite come to pass. Macri's audacious hijacking of Perón's image to boost his own message of efficiency and non-partisanship showed his determination to woo all Argentinians to his political project. Even so, at the time of the unveiling, only a few weeks before the election, he was considered unlikely to win.

In the event, he won the presidential run-off not so much on his merits but thanks to dissatisfaction with the government of CFK. The vote against CFK's chosen successor had more to do with weariness and alarm at the levels of antagonism in society than with unhappiness with the concrete results of the Kirchners' 12 years in government.

The successive Kirchner governments left behind a significantly better economy than the one they inherited. According to the World Bank income per capita rose from US$3,640 in 2003 to US$14,160 in 2013. Economist Mark Weisbrot writes that independent measures recorded a massive 80 per cent fall in poverty. According to the International Monetary Fund, unemployment fell from more than 17.2 of the workforce to 6.9 per cent. Social protection was expanded with the creation of a universal basic state pension; child benefits meant informal and poor workers had a way of ensuring education and nutrition for their children. Inequality was reduced from a Gini coefficient of 53.5 in 2003 to 43.6 in 2011, one of the few countries to reduce inequality in the same period. The country's road networks have been modernized and more new cars put on them than ever before, airports have been refurbished and millions have travelled abroad.

Although national statistics were compromised in Argentina, the World Bank drew on its own research to state that 'Argentina was the top performer in the region in reducing poverty and boosting shared prosperity between 2004 and 2008. Incomes of the bottom 40 per cent grew at an annualized rate of 11.8 per cent compared to overall average income growth of 7.6%. This trend continued but slowed after 2008. As of 2014, 12.7 per cent lived in poverty – defined as living on under $4 a-day. A third of the population lives on between 4 and 10 dollars a day and remains at risk of falling back into poverty.'[1]

Yet the polarization of society overshadowed the economic gains and the government's strategy of dividing different interests into opposing factions made everyone lose sight of what was gained. And people voted for change. Macri succeeded in making 'change' a feel-good generic promise, without concrete content. He offered to change the things people didn't like about CFK's government, but he didn't say how. His happy optimism ("the happiness revolution is starting" was one of his campaign slogans) was boosted by the Peronist candidate Daniel Scioli's scaremongering campaign. Instead of talking up the achievements he was inheriting from CFK, he concentrated on speculating on the terrible things Macri might do. Even though he was proved right, it was off-putting. It left Macri free to be positive, to offer the hope of change and to be as vague as he wished.

A country split down the middle

On 22 November 2015 Macri won the presidency by fewer than 700,000 votes, revealing a country split down the middle. But his electoral alliance also won the governorship of Buenos Aires province, a Peronist stronghold and the country's most important political district. His party held on to the local government of the city of Buenos Aires after two terms in office. It was a convincing win, even though his party and allies had a minority in both Congress and Senate.

The election results show an even split between progressive and more conservative forces in Argentinian society. It is an interesting result because it is not explained simply by party politics and has more to do with attitudes to power and the role of the market. Only time will tell whether it follows the same contours as the 'the rift', the much talked about *grieta*, the term used to describe the bitter differences that arose within society, even within families and groups of friends, where some supported and others criticised the Kirchner governments.

The day after the election it seemed that the rift might reflect social divisions that were most visible in the 1970s. The day's editorial in the right wing *La Nación* newspaper read 'No more vengeance'. It claimed that 'the election of a new government is a good moment to put an end to the lies about the 1970s and the current violations of human rights'. This was referring to the trials and prison sentences being meted out to those who took part in the state's crimes against humanity during the last dictatorship (1976-1982). The editors clearly felt that their call for interfering with the rule of law would find sympathetic ears in the new government.

Public repudiation of *La Nación's* stance was overwhelming, backed by the paper's own workforce, other journalists, and society at large. It suggests that perhaps the rift can be narrowed through a shared respect for the law. Macri's muted response was to say that the courts should have total independence to pursue justice. The incident showed that the support for justice set in motion by Néstor Kirchner's annulment of the amnesty laws protecting those accused of violations of human rights has become common sense above politics.

President Macri has repeatedly said that he will strengthen the rule of law and show respect for the division of powers, and that was part of his appeal. Yet as soon as he won the election and failed to agree how to conduct the handover of power with CFK, he asked the state attorney in charge of electoral matters to terminate CFK's mandate at midnight of the day before he took office. His request was accepted so that instead of negotiating a handover, he used the judicial system to resolve a political dispute. More worryingly, this was the same state attorney who felt unable to continue proceedings against Macri within days of his election in a case where he was suspected of tapping the phones of political and personal rivals. That leaves open a mere 213 legal proceedings in which Macri stands accused. The charges against him include 'fraud and illicit association', 'abuse of power and violation of the duties of an elected representative', and 'falsifying public documents'. There has been no comment in the mainstream media on the contradiction between these charges and his promises to take on corruption and be a staunch defender of the rule of law.

He has shown his lack of interest for due process by announcing game-changing policies by executive decree. In the first weeks of his mandate he bypassed Congress to reduce taxes on agribusiness and industrial exports and to float the peso freely for the first time in four years, leading the currency to devalue by a third in a day.[2] He tried to appoint Supreme Court judges by decree, something only dictatorships had considered doing before. He shut down the media regulator brought into existence by the Media Law of 2009 and posted a line of military police to stop its employees entering the building. Within a month he had announced increases in electricity and water that multiplied previous bills several times over. He put the country under a state of emergency as a response to 'complex and organized crime'.

In foreign policy, it was revealed that the week before formally taking power, the presumptive minister for Finances, Alfonso Prat Gay, had called US Treasury Secretary Jacob J. Lew to present him with Macri's economic plans, and the pair had what was reported as an 'auspicious' conversation. That would be like an elected UK government running economic policy past Germany's finance minister before presenting a budget to Parliament. The new government's understanding of national sovereignty seemed a touch shaky. But the store Macri sets by US influence in Argentina is long-standing and is visible in cables revealed through Wikileaks. In the past decade, he was recorded as urging the US ambassador to criticize CFK's government and be publicly 'tougher' on her measures. The ambassador replied 'that we will continue to seek a positive working relationship with the government of Argentina'. Macri saw no problem in inviting US intervention in national affairs, ignoring the abhorrent history of such meddling in the region. Journalist Santiago O'Donnell, in his book *Argenleaks*, records the bizarre spectacle of a US ambassador gently reminding Macri that it was his job, as the opposition, to contest the government's measures.

The first international task Macri's government undertook was settling with the 'holdout' hedge funds (the 'Vulture Funds') that were holding Argentina's debt payments hostage to a legal extortion process.[3] Ten weeks after coming to power, the Macri government agreed to pay US$4,65 billion to these bond holders.[4] To underline his position in foreign relations, the first international event that Macri attended was the World Economic Forum at Davos, the first time Argentina had sent a delegation in 12 years.

Home economics

If the economic agenda was driven by 'returning to the world' and accepting the conditions of international finance, economics nationally was similarly focused on ensuring the markets were freer to operate as they wished. First, exporters saw their taxes reduced, then it was the turn of mining companies. After freeing the currency and the consequent devaluation, people were told they were now free to buy 'up to 5 million dollars' at a time, an indication of how little Macri's economic team understands the lives of the average citizen.

One of the government's first priorities was to fire state employees who were thought to be supportive of the previous government, or in areas of work that were not a priority, such as preventative health and sexual education. In Macri's first month in power, nearly

20,000 people were fired from national, provincial and municipal levels of government across the country.[5] By March 2016 over 140,000 people had lost their jobs, just under half in state positions.[6]

Workers dismissed from public office were told at first that they were drawing a salary but not working; when they protested that they did in fact carry out their work, they were told that their informal contracts were not acceptable as a form of state employment. Yet many workers have reported that their work and contracts were not reviewed, but only their political sympathies were noted. There was no discernible process and certainly no time to make an informed judgement, and no attempt to involve those affected by the decisions.

Argentina has lived through many economic adjustments, and people expected some pain in return for a more predictable economy. Yet along with growing

Mauricio Macri speaking to the Annual Conference of the Argentine Institute of Financial Executives (IAEF), May 2012
Flickr. Creative Commons Attribution 2.0 Generic

unemployment the inflation they thought would be tamed gathered momentum. In June 2016 the Finance Minister admitted that inflation was near 45 per cent. As jobs were lost and prices rose in the first half of 2016, the government promised that the shock of adjustment wouldn't last, and by the second semester everything would be well. In the second semester they said it might take longer, but not how long.

When Macri became president at the head of a right-wing coalition of parties, it was widely reported that his ascent was the first time a right-wing politician representing the interests of the landed and financial oligarchy had reached the presidency by democratic means. In the past they had resorted to coups instead. The majority of the population is slowly discovering that, despite being elected, the government is indeed ruling for the few who were desperate to be able to buy five million dollars with their pesos.

People have mobilized for their lost jobs, against the rising fares and services, but the social response has as yet failed to coalesce around a defined leadership or set of demands. Large protests have taken place but have met with only passing mentions in the press, reducing their impact. The discrepancy between what is reported in the mainstream media and in alternative and citizen-driven outlets grows larger by the day. It is more subtle than censorship; a small example is a front page of Clarín in August that reported long queues outside a bookshop as an expression of Argentinians' love of reading, which is very real. They simply failed to mention that the clearance sale was due to the bookshop having to close down due to the sudden rise in rent and services, along with thousands of other small shops.[7]

The ambivalence felt about the legacy of the Kirchner governments can perhaps be best seen in this leadership vacuum that has appeared where opposition to Macri's measures could be growing. Most people are directly affected by the price hikes, the lack of job prospects, the closing down of businesses. All the union confederations have come together, in an unprecedented show of unity. Yet there is no political leadership with a plan of opposition to the government's measures. Instead, Macri's government has been able to count on Peronist votes to get measures passed in Congress. Moreover, in the first year after CFK left power, the legacy of her tenure is being successfully buried under cases of corruption that make it impossible for the gains of the populist decade to be defended wholeheartedly.[8]

Anthropologist Sian Lazar is an acute observer of political mobilization in Argentina and proposes that one way to think about Macri's election win is to consider whether people belong to political, social or cultural organizations or whether their politics are a more individual expression.[9] For individual voters, who are also more subject to mass media messages, Macri brought the promise of freedom from the collective constraints defended by CFK. But with social organizations bereft of a unifying political leadership, and on the back foot about the populist shortcomings that Macri's government continually hammers home, those who didn't vote for Macri currently have no political representation.

A state of emergency?

In January 2016, Macri announced a state of emergency, to last for a year. It is formally intended to reinforce borders and airspace in the fight against organized crime and drug trafficking. In practice, it has been used by security forces to demand that people carry valid ID on them at all times for random stop and search. The blanket approach to security problems is disturbing and the climate of fear that it engenders is palpable. The police were already more often feared than turned to for help, and these measures reinforce a pervasive unease that Argentinians recognise from living under dictatorship. In June 2016 Macri repealed a law passed by President Alfonsín in 1984 designed to increase civilian control over the armed forces. The new powers Macri granted to the military were downplayed as changes in administrative organization, with ultimate control still with the Ministry of Defence, but the signal was unmistakable: more power and political recognition to the military.

The combination of these measures, added to rising prices of food, transport, electricity, and water and massive lay-offs, have sown fear in many Argentinians. The distress is compounded by a selective media blackout. The municipal workers in La Plata who were fired within days of President Macri winning power protested in front of their offices in December 2015. They were met with rubber bullets. The availability of phones and internet meant that their wounds were visible on social media, but the press did not report the incident. A few weeks later children in a slum in Buenos Aires were shot at with rubber bullets and some live ammunition by *gendarmes* (military police). They were rehearsing music for carnival in a community centre. The photos of their shocking wounds spread through social media and alternative press outlets.[10] The incident was covered by *La Nación* with a headline that read: 'Two gendarmes shot at'.[11] The Ministry of the Interior declared that it was not aware of the reason for the shootings and said it needed to 'investigate'.

Also within days of coming to power, the governor of Jujuy province arrested a high-profile community organizer, Milagros Sala. She had been a thorn in the side of the political elites in the region for years. She was detained on charges of disturbing the peace, for a protest she had been involved with for months. She remains in custody although according to Amnesty International, the charges against her amount to the criminalization of protest.[12] Meanwhile the press has been content to run stories accusing her, without evidence, of corruption which is was not part of the charges used to arrest her or keep her imprisoned.

The law is created...

One of Argentina's infamous proverbs is *'hecha la ley hecha la trampa'*, which translates roughly as 'when the law is created so is the loophole'. Respect for rules and the law is compromised by the widespread belief that 'everybody else is breaking them'. Macri's support is in part based on people wanting a more independent and transparent judiciary and the observance of the rule of law. But the actions of his government and allies have so far been diametrically opposed to the much needed respect for the law. Macri's party, *Propuesta Republicana*, Republican Proposal or PRO, presents itself as a modern, technocratic solution to the country's problems, where the republican tools of government, that is the rule of law, due process, transparency and independent powers are strengthened. Meanwhile Macri has made much political capital of accusations of corruption and dishonesty in the previous governments.

Yet one of the many problems with public accusations based on character (rather than proceedings initiated by the courts where crimes or misconduct are investigated) is that it also brings the focus on the probity and character of the accuser. Macri's claim that he is honest and transparent is not backed up by evidence. When asked point blank if his childhood friend Nicolás Caputo had ever won Buenos Aires city contracts (where Macri was the elected mayor), he categorically denied it. But journalists uncovered the fact that Caputo is the majority stakeholder in companies that have won multimillion contracts from the city authorities. There are many cases in the public domain that attest to Macri's disregard for truth, due process, the rule of law and national sovereignty. Historian Ezequiel Adamovsky has compiled a list of actions by Macri and those near him that contravene the law, and is sceptical that those who celebrate his victory as a way of strengthening institutions are genuine in their concerns.

Macri is not new to politics and is not an unknown quantity. He was mayor of Buenos Aires for two consecutive terms, elected in 2007 and again in 2011. He led the Autonomous City of Buenos Aires, to give it its official title, the wealthiest administrative unit in the country, with a Human Development Index closer to that of Japan than the rest of Argentina. According to the 2010 census it had 2,800,000 inhabitants. This may seem strange given that Buenos Aires is the third largest conurbation in Latin America, after Mexico City and Sao Paulo. It is explained by the artificial boundaries that separate the city from its suburbs: for most of its perimeter, only a ring road distinguishes the 'capital' from the 'province'. It is simply a convenient way of separating the wealthy capital from the mostly poor suburbs. This division means the city, rather like the City of London, has not grown in population in a hundred years and has consistently represented a grouping of the richest individuals and businesses in the country.

In spite of increasing the tax burden and achieving record tax collections in the city, Macri left the city finances with four times more debt than when he arrived. As far as can be ascertained, the extra loans did not go on major works but on running costs. The Human Rights Observatory for the capital noted that three times more was budgeted for Christmas decorations for the city centre than for all Housing and Social Inclusion projects. But this fact was just an aside in a report that showed how between 2011 and 2014 the budget for advertizing had tripled while social spending fell.

The Observatory has been one of the few organizations to systematically monitor the conduct of the capital's government. It also noted the dearth of media coverage of reports of serious human rights violations. The worst involved the *Unidad de Control del Espacio Público* (UCEP), the Unit for Controlling Public Spaces. UCEP was created by Macri in 2008 and one of its aims was to keep public space 'free of trespassers'. What this meant in practice was the violent eviction of homeless people and unauthorised settlements, with physical force used against women and children, property and documents burnt and destroyed, and those forcibly evicted being intentionally intimidated and injured. In a report by the Public Ombudsman, members of the UCEP admitted that it had carried out 444 of these 'operations'. While giving evidence in court, members of the UCEP revealed that Macri was aware of their activities, and in at least one case directly ordered it. In June 2015 he was acquitted of any charges, but members of the now disbanded UCEP were sentenced.

The effects of Macri's city government on the most vulnerable can also be seen in data on health in Buenos Aires. The rate of infant mortality has fluctuated in the city, while in the country as a whole it has decreased steadily in the same period. The overall rise in infant deaths in the capital since 2010 seems related to the inequality in health provision, with the poorer boroughs to the south of the city seeing rates more than double those of the wealthier north. In the south of the city over a third of inhabitants depend on (free) public provision, whereas in the city as a whole only 17 per cent of the population are not covered by private or employment-derived health services.[13] While Macri was quick to criticize the deplorable influence the Kirchners wielded over the national statistics office, there is very little independently verified information available to judge his performance in the city.

No time like the present

Since Macri has been president, all these trends have been accentuated: giving economic advantages to the richest, using violence against the poor and vulnerable, increasing inequality with price hikes and layoffs. The ongoing tragedy is that the fragile system of bureaucratic checks and balances that might protect ordinary people is lacking, as is a stable machinery of government that could deliver their rights.

As political scientists Carlos Gervasoni and Enrique Peruzzotti note, Néstor Kirchner and CFK enjoyed favourable conditions during their mandates to build up state capacities.[14] They enjoyed strong political leadership with simple or outright majorities in Congress; they could draw on increasing fiscal income from favourable commodity prices and an expanded tax base, and they strongly advocated support for the public sphere. And yet, the way they implemented their policies undermined the ongoing capacity of the state to provide economic and social development and the structures through which people could demand them.

The hope many placed on the new Macri government was to begin to remedy the historic weakness in Argentina's institutions of government. From the measures taken in the first six months of his government, there is little evidence that this is an aim of the new president or his team. Attempting to appoint High Court judges by decree, firing state workers with no transparent process, closing down the media regulator, giving more autonomy to the military, unleashing market forces overnight with no safety net: these have been the rapid policy changes that feel more like retaliation against specific actions of the previous governments than an attempt to build more transparency and legitimacy into the state.

The continuing emphasis on the corruption of the Kirchners is not matched by raising standards for judicial independence and best practice. The political thrust of new investigations, and the equally politically-motivated stalling or closing of others relating to current government officials is depressingly familiar.

Macri is comfortable appointing senior officials with proven records of acting against the interests of the country, such as the President of the Central Bank, Federico Sturzenegger. He remains accused of being part of a financial manoeuvre in 2001 to benefit banks at the taxpayers' expense, significantly worsening the financial meltdown at the time.[15] Although legal proceedings have been glacially slow, Sturzenegger has since been investigated for corruption by the courts and a Senate committee. He is not an exception. In June 2016 it was revealed that Vice-President Gabriela Michetti had not reported a break-in at her home the previous November where 245,000 pesos and 50,000 US dollars in cash were stolen. Much of the money she claims belonged to a foundation of which she is a trustee. The entire affair seemed less than transparent, and she has given various conflicting explanations, none of which really explain why she did not report the theft in the first place or why she might have a donation of that size in cash, at home.

By contrast, social activist Milagros Sala had been in prison for four months before the governor of Jujuy confirmed that she was being held on corruption charges. While double standards persist in investigating corruption, nothing can be said to have improved in the political uses of justice, and due process is in real jeopardy.

In the 'Who we are' section of the PRO's website it states that although PRO brings together different visions, 'we are united by an interest in the future, not the constant revision of the past'. The Kirchners' use of the past failed to create a national project that included everyone. But Macri's rule by decree has so far only benefited a wealthy minority and continues to widen social rifts. The lack of interest in the past is belied by government officials who have been promoting denialism of the crimes against humanity perpetrated by the last dictatorship.[16] The city's culture minister eventually resigned over his claim that 30,000 is a an inflated number of victims, but a few months later President Macri himself gave credence to doubters. These controversies point to political narratives that are not interested in facts and accuracy and instead reveal the deep political divisions that still exist in Argentina.

Moreover, basing new policies on reversing those established by the Kirchners and making blanket accusations of corruption does not amount to a credible plan of government. For a government that bases it legitimacy on economic management, in the first year of government it has overseen a contraction of GDP, inflation of 40 per cent and a larger deficit than in 2015. The investment they promised has not appeared and by their own standards, they have so far failed.[17] The economic improvements Macri promised for the first six months failed to materialise. He then promised that 'the second semester' would see recovery and improvement. Six months into his government, he kicked forward the possibility of reducing inflation to an indefinite point in the future.[18] He has reduced taxes, taken on more debt. Meanwhile the economic recovery promised after the adjustment is nowhere to be seen. Instead there is a growing social gap created by economic pain for many so that a few can buy millions of dollars.

Notes

1   http://www.worldbank.org/en/country/argentina/overview

2   http://www.bbc.com/mundo/noticias/2015/12/151217_argentina_fin_cepo_devaluacion_irm

3   http://www.newyorker.com/business/currency/a-good-week-for-vulture-funds

4   http://www.nytimes.com/2016/04/01/opinion/how-hedge-funds-held-argentina-for-ransom.html?_r=0

5   http://www.eldestapeweb.com/el-mapa-los-despidos-macri-n13771

6   http://www.pagina12.com.ar/diario/elpais/1-297874-2016-04-26.html

7   http://www.diarioregistrado.com/sociedad/por-la-crisis-cierra-una-libreria-pero-clarin-destaca-la--pasion--por-los-libros_a57c57aeeda77603d0f31bbbd

8   http://www.eldiplo.org/207-contra-el-ajuste/ajuste-sin-rebelion/

9   http://www.focaalblog.com/2016/03/17/sian-lazar-the-happiness-revolution-argentina-and-the-end-of-post-neoliberalism/

10 http://www.lavaca.org/notas/represion-en-bajo-flores-ninos-heridos-y-silencio-de-ministerio/

11 http://www.lanacion.com.ar/1866789-dos-gendarmes-fueron-baleados-en-un-operativo-en-la-villa-1-11-14

12 http://chequeado.com/el-explicador/seis-puntos-sobre-la-detencion-de-milagro-sala/

13 These figures are provided by a think tank connected to the Kirchners' party, the *Frente para la Victoria* - it would clearly be better if there were independent data to analyse.

14 Editors of 'Decada Ganada? Evaluando el legado del kirchnerismo.' http://www.utdt.edu/ver_novedad.php?id_novedad=1362&id_item_menu=442

15 http://www.pagina12.com.ar/diario/economia/2-289193-2015-12-29.html

16 https://www.theguardian.com/world/2016/aug/29/argentina-denial-dirty-war-genocide-mauricio-macri

17 http://www.eldiplo.org/207-contra-el-ajuste/ajuste-sin-rebelion/

18 http://chequeado.com/hilando-fino/como-cambio-macri-su-discurso-del-segundo-semestre/

Latin America Bureau (LAB)

LAB is an independent charitable organization, based in London, which provides news, analysis and information on Latin America, reporting consistently from the perspective of the region's poor, oppressed or marginalized communities and social movements. LAB brings an alternative, critical awareness and understanding of Latin America to readers throughout the English-speaking world.

LAB is widely known for its books and operates a website, updated daily, in which it carries news and analysis on Latin America and reports from our partners and correspondents in the region (www.lab.org.uk).

LAB books (over 100 titles) can be purchased from http://developmentbookshop.com/publishers/latin-america-bureau (the website shop of Practical Action Publishing).

Recent Lab Titles

K by Bernardo Kucinski. The story of a father who searches for his daughter, 'disappeared' during the military dictatorship in Brazil.

Rosa of the Wild Grass - The Story of a Nicaraguan Family by Fiona Macintosh (2016). This fascinating and deeply moving personal and family chronicle brings alive the tumult of events over more than 50 years in a way no textbook of contemporary politics could achieve.

Brazil Inside Out: People, Politics and Culture by Jan Rocha and Francis McDonagh. 2nd edition (2016). The first of LAB's new Inside Out series for the thoughtful visitor, tourist or student.

Other titles in the LAB Special Report series:

Brazil Under the Workers Party: from Utopia to Despair by Sue Branford (2015)
The Nicaragua Grand Canal: Economic Miracle or Folie de Grandeur? by Russell White (2015)